Meet Me at the Bakery

My Journey through Grief and Back to Life

Priscilla Boos

CROSSBOOKS
PUBLISHING

CrossBooks™
A Division of LifeWay
1663 Liberty Drive
Bloomington, IN 47403
www.crossbooks.com
Phone: 1-866-879-0502

First published by CrossBooks 5/07/2012

ISBN: 978-1-4627-1692-0 (e)
ISBN: 978-1-4627-1691-3 (sc)
ISBN: 978-1-4627-1709-5 (hc)

Library of Congress Control Number: 2012907200

Printed in the United States of America

This book is printed on acid-free paper.

Certain stock imagery © Thinkstock.
Any people depicted in stock imagery provided by Thinkstock are models,
and such images are being used for illustrative purposes only.

Meet Me
at the Bakery

Dedication

To Bill – without whom I would have missed out on an incredible life adventure. He was my friend, confidant, encourager, life partner, and lover. His quick wit and dry sense of humor kept us all laughing to the very end. And, his deep faith sustained him (and us) through the worst of this journey called "life."

To Sharon Baker – who so strongly believed that my story must be told, she gave me the title for the book.

To Peggy Kellum – whose persistent reassurance, from the first few words I penned, kept me forging forward. Her honest feedback helped me stay focused and encouraged me to dig deep to find the words to tell my story.

To my brother, John – whose support has meant the world to me! He offered me affirmation, and asserted that I needed to complete the book so it could help and bless others. He is the best brother anyone could ever ask for!

To Viktoria Gotting – whose path God detoured for a bit so she could be with Bill and me at the end, and who officiated so beautifully at his funeral. She is a dear, trusted friend who is destined for greatness in the Kingdom of God.

To Mary Luehrmann and Carol Clarke – whose wisdom in grammar and storytelling helped me complete the final editing. They are new friends with whom I have been blessed, and the encouragement and feedback they offered were invaluable to me.

To Anita Christopher – a member of "the club" who I met just three months after Bill died. She is a dear and treasured friend who understands the unique challenges of having lost the spouse you deeply love, and whose fearless approach to life helped me engage socially again.

Contents

Introduction

*S*ometimes life throws curves at you that you can't, or wouldn't want to, anticipate and your entire world is rocked to its very core. What do you do when everything you've built comes crashing down around you? How do you handle having the rug pulled right out from under you, and entering the darkest, loneliest place gripped by debilitating, paralyzing fear? How can you find your way back? And back to what? 'Cause life as you knew it is completely gone. I have been there, and I am back. With the grace and love of God; the support of family, coworkers, and friends; and help from grief counseling, I have survived. I have not only survived, I have overcome!

This is my story—the story of my journey with my husband, Bill, his illnesses, my passage through the valley of the shadow of death, and my return to life. And, praise God, I have emerged stronger for having taken that journey. Yes, things are different. I am profoundly altered, yet I am the same. I laugh again, but I cry much easier. I am more understanding of people's struggles, and my heart reaches out to them without judgment. I know what is important, and I don't sweat the small stuff. And, life is good again. Really good! I am grateful for every breath I take, every step I walk, and every second of life with which I am blessed. Thank God from whom all blessings flow!

I want you to know that you, too, can survive the most devastating loss. My prayer is that my story will bless and encourage you, and give you hope that there truly is life after death. And, not only for the person who has gone to be with the Lord, but for the surviving spouse as well. My journey is unique, as is yours. But, if by sharing my own experience I can help you find the courage to survive yours, I am happy to have taken the painful journey back to those dark, lonely places.

The Beginning

ill and I had one of those love stories that is so rare and so special that it is hard to put into words. And, the thing that made it so amazing is that our love affair lasted for thirty-nine years.

On January 9, 1971, I met Bill on a blind date arranged by my cousin, Jimmie, who was also Bill's friend, and it was "connection at first sight." I can still remember the exact moment that our connection occurred. We were in Port Jefferson on Long Island and before crossing the street, he looked at me, held his hand out, and asked, "Are you game?" I remember smiling back, and though I do not remember my exact reply to him, I took his hand and we crossed the street. Something happened at the moment that we clasped hands, and I cannot explain it, but I knew our journey together had begun. I went home from that date and told my family I had met the man I was going to marry. He went home and told his mother he was going to marry me. We both just knew! On our second date one week later, Bill asked me to marry him, and I said, "Yes." We were married on October 2, 1971, and thirty-nine years, two children, and six grandchildren later, he lay dying and my world was coming to an agonizing, crashing end.

Our Life

*B*ill was one of those guys who had an impact on people. Physically large and strong (he was 6'3" and rarely weighed less than 250 pounds), there was nothing he could not do. He was confident and fearless. We had been married just a couple of years when he chased a bank robber in Mineola, NY. When he caught up with the man, Bill knocked him down, and held him on the ground until the police arrived. He received a letter of commendation from the bank manager for that brave act. However, in true "Bill style," he did not keep the letter and never told anyone but me about that experience. Bill just never liked being the center of attention. Besides, he believed that that's just what you do! Another time he single-handedly lifted an old executive desk (you know, the ones made of real, solid wood) and carried it up several flights of stairs to its new location. Everyone at that office was amazed! Until I met Bill, I did not know that anyone could do things like that!

Bill was large and he definitely was strong. But, he was also a gentle man. He could carry that heavy desk up several flights of stairs, yet hold a tiny wounded bird in his hands with the utmost care and tenderness. Bill was my "gentle giant."

Although Bill was out of his element in a roomful of people, he would listen to the conversation around him and at the right moment, he would interject a word or two that was so unbelievably funny, the entire room would roar with hysterical laughter. I loved that about him! He had a wit that no one I have ever met could match, and he kept us all laughing until the very end. He could think quicker than most people and I always admired that about him, being secretly jealous that I was not given that gift.

One time, I commented to him that his hairline was receding. "It's not receding, Pris" he retorted, "It's retreating!" And, yes, we both had a good laugh once again. That's just how our life was. And, it was really good!

Two things gave Bill more joy than he could ever express—the birth of our son, Joe, and the birth of our daughter, Vicki, three years later. He could not have been a more proud, happy dad! He loved getting on all fours when Joe was little, and riding him around the house on his back. He would do goofy things like taking the light bulb out of a flashlight and putting it in his nostril to make it look like he had a bubble coming out. That would make Joe laugh loud and long. I would have to tell him, "Bill, don't make him laugh!" because it would cause Joe to have an asthma attack. However, there is nothing like the happy squeals of a child laughing, and I couldn't help but laugh along as I chastised him!

When Vicki came along, Bill would do little skits for her with her dolls. She still remembers her dolls "dancing" together and "talking" to each other. He loved to dance with Vicki, and he would put her little feet on his huge 13-1/2 EEE shoes and dance her around the living room. Then he would pick her up, and hold her cheek to cheek while he continued their dance. I do not know who enjoyed that more—him or her! He was content and happy with his family, and emotionally, the best he would ever be.

Life as a family was not without its ups and downs, but we had a foundation of faith on which our family was built. And, the kids did have a safe, secure home in which to grow up. There was also lots of love and laughter in the house. Sometimes the bantering between us went on for the longest time, and the love between us grew steady and strong.

It was very hard on me when the kids grew up and left our home, but for Bill, it was devastating. Many times on a holiday he would say, "I miss the kids, Pris. I want them here with us." I would assure him that Joe would be with us later and Vicki would be calling us from New Jersey. He would always say the same thing, "No. I want them here, little again." It was not until Vicki and our three granddaughters lived with us the last three years of his life that he truly enjoyed the holidays again, especially Christmas.

Bill battled life-long chronic, severe depression and anxiety that affected every area of his life. I learned early on in our marriage that things that were easy for most people to handle overwhelmed Bill. As we faced life's challenges and difficulties throughout the years, Bill allowed life to beat him down. He responded by emotionally shutting down, and that was hard for me to experience. I discovered that as I became stronger facing life's challenges, he became more fearful and anxious. He only felt safe in our home with me. The last five years or so were especially difficult. He became very reclusive, and could only go to work and back home again. We did not socialize very much and his anxiety overtook him whenever anyone came into the house, or whenever he left it. I was determined to be a haven for him as long as he needed, and he was so very grateful for that.

Bill Gets Sick

*I*n January 2004, Bill and I embarked on a new venture: to build a house in Katy, Texas. The kids were grown and with their own families, and this house was the place Bill and I were going to grow old together. I had found the floor plan online, and asked him to take a look at the model with me. So, one weekend we drove from Houston to Katy to see the house. He immediately loved it, and we signed the contract on the spot. One thing about Bill—it took an act of Congress to get him to try anything new, but if he felt it was right, he went for it! That's what he did when he met me, and that is what he did when we moved from New York to Texas in 1980.

Bill was an all or nothing kind of guy. The middle of the road was not a comfortable place for him. There was no gray area in his world. Everything was black and white—period. I once teased him because his two favorite female singers were Mama Cass Elliot and Karen Carpenter. One ate herself to death and the other starved herself to death. He laughed at this observation about him, and realized it was such a perfect example of the enigma that he was!

By June 2004, our house was ready and we set a date for the closing. A week before we were to close, Bill developed a sudden heart problem—tachycardia and arrhythmia. It was so severe that medication did not help, and he wound up having an ablation done on his heart. He almost missed the house closing and was released from the hospital just a couple of hours before our appointment with the title company. At the time, I thought *that* was stressful. Little did I realize that that was the beginning of one of the most unbelievable journeys we would ever take, and that our world as we knew it would forever change.

We settled into our new home and Bill seemed to do much better with his depression. I attributed that to the large windows and God's beautiful, healing sunshine pouring into every room of the house. It was not long, however, before his depression and anxiety took hold of him again. And, he became both quarrelsome and reclusive. He stopped opening the blinds, preferring to use artificial light. He was very withdrawn and angry. It was a very difficult time for me, but I filled my time with work, friends, and activities.

Bill had been diagnosed with emphysema some time in 1995/1996, and he managed it well for many years. Then in 2004, things seemed to physically fall apart for him. He not only developed more heart problems, but I noticed other things that were not right. For example, he would be driving down a street he had driven on many times before, but he suddenly did not know where he was. He was forgetting things—whole situations and events, not just pieces of information. We knew something was wrong but could not pinpoint the cause of the problem. In 2005, Bill totaled his car because he lost consciousness while driving. He was admitted to the hospital and was put through a whole barrage of tests, but no reason was ever discovered to explain why he had passed out. As time progressed, he started to see more doctors—a pulmonologist, then a cardiologist, and finally, a neurologist. I noticed he would drive between two lanes on the road, and when I brought that to his attention, he would get upset. He wouldn't be upset with me, but with the fact that something was happening to him that was unknown, uncontrollable, and frightening. He seemed to be getting more tired, and when he returned home from work each evening, he could barely make it to the bedroom to lie down. He would be physically bowed over, and would have to use his C-Pap machine to get air into his lungs. I was very concerned, and I watched him closely, making mental notes of the "little" things I was seeing. I ensured that he went to all his doctor visits and faithfully took all his medications. However, I felt so helpless...

Vicki Comes Home

*I*n July 2007, Vicki and her family left New Jersey and moved in with us. She had been gone for ten years and she missed her family and her life in Texas and wanted to come back home. It was just what Bill and I needed! We had our daughter home again with our three beautiful granddaughters who brought more light and joy to us than they will ever know! And, Bill was able to rise above his depression and anxiety…even just a little.

The Journey Continues

*O*ne thing is sure…no matter how much Bill tried to feel good, he just couldn't quite get there. I watched it become more and more difficult for him to go to work every morning. And when I broached the subject of his retiring, he said, "Not yet, Pris. I don't want to retire earlier than my father did. I have to work until I'm at least sixty-two." He was only sixty years old, and I wondered how he would be able to continue his work routine for two more years. However, he had the right to make his own decision, and I made it my mission to watch him from afar. You know… like when the kids are little and they want to do things their own way, so you let them walk to their friend's house a few doors down, but you hide behind the bushes to be sure they are safe. That is what I did for Bill.

More symptoms started to surface, and one night while we were sound asleep, Bill suddenly catapulted out of bed. He was literally flying through the air, and when he landed, he hit the wall on the other side of the bed, knocked the lamp off the nightstand, pulled his C-Pap machine down to the floor, and gave himself a big knot on his head. The crashing sounds woke me as I saw this play out, and I jumped up and ran to him. He was on the floor, stunned and disoriented. I asked him, "Are you okay?" He said he was, so then I asked him, "What happened?" He said he didn't know. I then asked if he was dreaming and maybe he jumped out of the bed, but he said he didn't think so. I helped him get up, and he sat on the side of the bed while I cleaned up the mess in the room. When I was sure he was okay, I teased him and asked him if he was trying to be one of the Flying Wallenda's! We both laughed, but I could tell he was really troubled. I made a mental "note to self" and filed it with the other "hmmmm's" under "What is happening to Bill?"

About a month or so later, Bill woke me up saying, "Pris, help me." He could barely form the words. Again, I jumped up, and within a few seconds, he was having a grand mal seizure. I flew through the house and got my daughter, who came running into the bedroom. What a blessing it was to have Vicki with us! I was able to observe first-hand, and for the first time, just what an amazing and outstanding nurse she is! She immediately kicked into nurse mode and firmly told me, "Mom, get dressed, then call an ambulance." I thought that I should call the ambulance first and then get dressed, feeling that at least they would already be on the way as I changed my clothes. Vicki explained, very calmly but purposefully, that they would be here rather quickly and I should be dressed when they arrived so I could go along. The explanation made sense, and I did as I was told. Vicki was right, too! The whole time Vicki talked to me, her eyes never left Bill. She stood there comforting him, reassuring him, keeping him safe, and being ready to take whatever action might be necessary. Her voice was soothing but authoritative, and she knowingly answered my questions while she cared for Bill. The ambulance came and Bill was admitted to the hospital for more tests.

These scenarios became the norm. Bill continued to have grand mal seizures, some of which lasted for ten minutes or more. One really bad one lasted for sixteen minutes! It was SO hard to see him writhing on the floor like that! He also had had several strokes, and TIA's (transient ischemic attacks) had starting coming regularly. It was very frightening both for him and for me. Even with a lot of medication, the seizures and strokes continued. Bill was in and out of the hospital having the same barrage of tests each time, but no reason was determined for the problems that had surfaced. It was so frustrating both for his doctors and for us!

In June of 2008, Bill just could not work anymore because the seizures and strokes were occurring quite often, and each one took a little more from him. It was difficult for him to walk because he was so off balance, his driving was dangerous and he voluntarily gave it up, he kept forgetting where he was, and he was scared. He had also developed dementia and that frightened him more than anything else. On several occasions, Bill commented to me that he was not afraid to die, but he was really afraid to live. The one thing he feared above all was that he would get to the place where he did not recognize me or his children and grandchildren. He remembered my mother's journey with Alzheimer's. She had lost her entire memory and all relationships, as well. She did not know anyone, not even her children. That was a place that gripped his very soul with sheer terror. I kept reassuring him that I would be right there with him—protecting and caring for him, no matter what happens. That comforted him, and in doing so, comforted me, too.

Finally, during one hospital stay in February 2009 his doctor told me the words I dreaded hearing more than anything in this entire world: "If Bill continues to decline at the current rate, he has no more than six months to a year to live." Thus began the beginning of the end…

Life and Fear

*B*ill and I had promised each other years ago that we would be completely honest with each other if we ever received bad news regarding our mortality. And, we affirmed that promise through the years. So, when Bill asked me what the doctor had said, I had to tell him the truth. I told him as gently as I could, but I did give him the prognosis. He was visibly shaken and stunned, and he cried. We both did a lot of crying along the way (something new for Bill), and I came to understand how utterly devastating the proverbial storms of life can be. I felt tossed and thrown from all directions, and wasn't at all sure I would be able to survive this. I felt as if I would drown in the sea of fear, feeling completely overwhelmed by the huge burden I was bearing, and the thought of what lay ahead. I was grateful for my faith because my spiritual anchor held—and it held strong! I kept wondering, and verbalizing, how people who do not know the Lord get through these situations. And, I truly do not know. What do they hang on to when they are barely hanging on? I am unable to answer that question.

Knowing your days are actually numbered is a very sobering realization. Scripture does tell us that, but the reality of that truth hit Bill and me between the eyes. All the fear and anxiety Bill ever felt in his life surfaced and consumed him. He struggled with not earning an income, he worried that I would be unable or unwilling to handle things as he got worse and that I would leave, and he was greatly afraid of the road ahead of him. As a result, he became suicidal. I had to hire a caretaker to watch over him, so I could be sure he would still be there when I returned home from work each evening. It was a very difficult time for both of us.

It is during these difficult times that you realize how important the spiritual teaching is that you received as a child and throughout your life. That knowledge and the faith that comes from relying on God and seeing Him work on your behalf, gives you the strength to face and endure these situations. I had learned early on to seek God for guidance and direction since my father had passed away when I was just a teenager. In fact, he died right on the day of my sixteenth birthday. Not having an earthy father to talk to, forced me to go to my heavenly Father when I was faced with life's challenges. So, it was a natural thing for me to pray and trust God to guide us and to take care of us through these trying times. That is simply what I do—what I've always done.

Good in the Midst of Bad

*Y*ou know, in every situation, no matter how bad, there is always some good. The good for Bill came in the form of three precious little girls—our granddaughters who were living with us. Oh, how Bill loved those girls! They just lit up his life! Each one is completely different from the other; but together, they filled his heart with lots of love and joy. Ashlyn, our eldest granddaughter, is a "social butterfly." An outgoing, friendly child, her smile lights up the room. She is also a very sensitive, loving, caring child. Samantha, our middle granddaughter, is quiet and thoughtful. She never speaks above a whisper, and is unassuming and reserved. Like Bill, however, she can bring the house down with just one word. And, she loves deeply and gives the best hugs, too! Kristina (Tina), the youngest, has more personality in her little body than any child you will ever meet! And, she and Bill bonded more deeply and profoundly than anything any of us had ever experienced or witnessed before. She wasn't even two years old when she came to live with us. Even before she could talk, if you asked her who her buddy was, she would point to Bill. He just *melted* when she did that. They had a connection that was almost spiritual. It went way beyond the normal grandfather/granddaughter relationship. Everyone knew it, and everyone enjoyed watching them interact with each other. Their love for each other was nothing short of amazing.

When Tina could talk, she refused to call Bill "Poppy" as the others did. To her, he was "Buddy" because he was her best buddy. And she meant that! She would not allow any of the other grandchildren to call him "Buddy," either. He was *her* Buddy and no one else's! She was with him all day with the caretaker, and she and Bill watched Sponge Bob together every day. They were "best buddies" and they watched out for each other. She was utterly loyal to her Buddy and she loved him unconditionally.

Bill had an "addiction" to a brand of ice cream that is made in Brenham, Texas—Blue Bell. He absolutely loved it, and ate it every chance he could. It was a serious addiction. He could sit with a spoon and the half-gallon container of whatever flavor we had and could polish off the entire thing. Many times, I would return home from work to hear Bill say he was not hungry for dinner. When I checked the freezer, I would find that all the Blue Bell was gone. I would get upset with him when he did that, because I at least wanted him to try to eat healthy. Nevertheless, my words fell on "deaf ears!" Tina knew what had happened to the ice cream, but she never snitched on him. To the contrary, she would tell me, "Nanny, you leave my Buddy alone!" In her eyes, he could do no wrong. She always fiercely defended him and Bill loved her depth of loyalty. He used to tell me that he was embarrassed by the fact that his best friend was a toddler.

One afternoon I left work early because I was so utterly exhausted. When I got home, I told Tina and the caretaker that I was going to lie down. "You be quiet, Nanny!" Tina demanded. "My Buddy is sleeping!" "Yes ma'am!" I replied, and I laughed as I entered the bedroom. I had been chastised by a three-year-old! Tina was very protective of Bill, and he reveled in the love that poured out of her little heart into his. They were Best Buddies and nothing could, or would, ever change that.

Bill Declines

*B*ill fought hard to be self-sufficient. Even though walking was a challenge and forbidden, in true Bill style, he continued to try to walk. He fell a lot and was in and out of the hospital and rehabilitation facilities, and his dementia continued to get worse. His thought process became irrational and he would do things that did not make sense. For example, he would turn the icemaker off in the freezer. He thought that if he did not turn it off, the ice would overflow and melt, and we would have a puddle on the floor. I tried to explain to him that there is a sensor in the icemaker and that the sensor automatically shuts the icemaker off when the receptacle is full. Even if the sensor failed and the ice cubes overflowed, they would overflow into the freezer where they would remain frozen. He just could not grasp that concept and we had several "discussions" about it every time we had no ice. We finally agreed that he would not turn the icemaker off and that I would clean up the mess when there was a puddle on the floor. Eventually Bill forgot about the icemaker and there was peace again in our home.

Bill also lost his short-term memory. He would ask the same question repeatedly, forgetting that he not only had asked it but that I had answered it. One Saturday afternoon I gave him lunch and when he had finished eating, I picked up the dish and empty soda can, and brought them to the kitchen sink. As soon as those items were out of his sight, he asked me, "Pris, have I had lunch today?" I told him he had just eaten lunch: a ham and cheese sandwich, some chips, and a soda. He looked at me with a puzzled expression on his face then made a joke to cover up his embarrassment. "Hmmm, I guess that's why I'm not hungry, huh?" I smiled sheepishly and gave him a hug.

Then, one Sunday afternoon in March 2009, Bill had another stroke. Against my ranting and raving, he insisted on taking the trash out. He hadn't been feeling well that day and he did not look right at all to me but there was no stopping him. He felt so useless by that point that he insisted he needed to do this. "It's all I have left, Pris," he said. "I've lost everything else. I need to do this." I hated those moments. They were so hard for me to manage emotionally because I wanted to keep him completely safe, but I also wanted him to feel useful and that he was a continuing part of our life. I felt that no matter what decision I made, it would ultimately be the wrong one. However, I did the best I could, feeling that as long as my motivation was to do the right thing for Bill, and that my heart was in the right place, I didn't need to feel guilty. I made the best decisions I could along the way and tried not to second-guess myself. I forced myself to keep looking forward and to prepare for the next challenge we would have to face. Therefore, I compromised that day. I backed off from insisting that he not take the trash out, but I asked Ashlyn to watch him as he did. A few minutes later, Ashlyn came running to me to tell me, "Poppy fell and he's hurt. He can't get up, Nanny." I ran out to the driveway and found Bill lying in the street. He was hurt, and unable to get up. Bill was in pain and bleeding from several places. I tried to lift him, but I could not even move him. I asked Ashlyn to get her mother, thinking that together Vicki and I could lift Bill, but we just were not strong enough. Then, as we contemplated what to do, a car came down the street. The man driving the car stopped and asked me if we needed help. I told him, "Yes... please..." He was so kind. He got out of his car and helped us get Bill up and into the house. I thanked the man profusely, and he told me he did not know why he was on our street other than he had made a wrong turn but that he was glad he had. He was very happy he could help us out. I will be forever grateful to that man, whose name I do not even know, for having a heart that reached out to assist us. I couldn't help but think about how wonderfully God was taking care of us just as He had always done, and I whispered a quick prayer of thanks. Bill was badly hurt from the fall and he was in a lot of pain. We called an ambulance and once again, he was in the hospital. He had a broken wrist, a broken ankle, lacerations, abrasions, and marked weakness on his left side. His dementia was also worse and he was irrational. He spent one week in the hospital and three weeks in a rehabilitation facility until he was finally able to come home.

Shortly after that incident, Bill fell again in the house and broke several ribs. Keeping him safe became a huge challenge for me, and watching him decline was more painful and heart wrenching than words can ever describe. Fear gripped me in the very depths of my soul: the fear that he would die, and the fear that he would live, lingering for a long time in this declining, depressing, debilitating state. For me, it was a lose/lose situation, and I struggled greatly with it. I knew that either way, my heart was destined to be broken. And, broken it was! I was never free of that pain. I had become the sole support of the family, and I had to keep working while bearing this enormous burden. Also, while all of this was going on with Bill, my mother was quickly failing from end-stage Alzheimer's. Things eventually got so bad that I did not know if my mother or Bill would go first, but I knew it would be close. I just hoped they would both not die on the same day. I did not know how I would survive all this. But, I completely trusted God's grace and mercy, and relied on the strength I received and kept going. Family, friends, and coworkers hovered closely, and they rallied 'round me on the especially bad days. I was barely able to keep things together, and the strength those hugs, cards, calls, and e-mails gave me is what carried me through. I cried a lot, and barely hung on by a tiny, thin thread. I sought counseling and had to take medication. I was depleted physically, mentally, and emotionally. Everyone noticed how tired I looked and many people kept telling me to take care of myself. It was only after Bill died that I realized how much of a toll all this had taken on me.

The one thing I counted on was the prayers of those who knew us and cared about us. I could feel God's strength from those prayers, and sometimes when I thought I could not go on, I could feel His peace. It was even hard for me to breathe, and I was always exhausted. Concentrating on work was a huge challenge, but I hung on. Sometimes I would tell myself, *just get through the next minute; Bill needs you—just one more minute, Pris.* A lot of people commented about how strong I was and I assured them that it was not my strength, but God's that was getting me through. Experiencing such miraculous strength was new to me because I have always been an independent, self-sufficient person. It was truly an amazing thing for me to realize.

I learned an important lesson through this, and that is that God wants to carry us through these hard places. All we have to do is allow Him to love and care for us. What an amazing lesson this was for me to learn! Sometimes, I would envision myself laying my head on the Lord's chest and having His arms enfold around me, holding and comforting me, and bringing me peace. That visual got me through when I just did not have it in me to go on one second longer. That image, and the strength from the many prayers that people raised on our behalf, are what sustained me.

In a very short time, Bill had gone from being a healthy, vibrant, strong man to being dependent on a cane, then a walker, and finally a wheelchair. He was suffering with COPD (Chronic Obstructive Pulmonary Disease), seizures, strokes, peripheral neuropathy with numbness in his legs and hands, dementia, weakness, and peripheral arterial disease. He was off balance and in constant pain—a deep pain that worsened with each passing day. He was also losing his hearing and his eyesight. He was on eighteen different medications. He could barely manage what was happening to him, and he talked about suicide all the time. I begged him not to go through with that because he would leave a devastating legacy for me, his children, and his grandchildren. I assured him that he would forever alter all those lives knowing their Dad/Poppy took his own life. I asked him if he really wanted to do that. He said, "No," but he told me the thought was always there.

Then, one night something happened that completely changed Bill, and our lives were altered once again.

Bill's Vision/Experience

*O*n June 28, 2009, Bill woke up with a strange expression on his face and he was visibly shaken. When I asked him what was wrong, he told me that something had happened to him during the night, and he was not sure if he had actually experienced it, or if he had dreamed it. He went on to explain that he suddenly found himself in what he perceived to be Heaven. He described it as looking like old town London as portrayed in the Scrooge movies. Bill loved the Scrooge movies because he loved the transformation that took place when Scrooge mended his ways. We owned every version of that movie and never missed watching all of them every Christmas. It drove the kid's nuts! Anyway, Bill said it was snowing, but it was not cold. It was nighttime, but there was light…and not from any light source we know. A being was with him who guided him through the town. Bill told me he could not see the being, but he could feel its presence and the two of them could converse. He could not tell from the voice whether the being was male or female. He felt extremely comfortable with this being, something Bill did not readily feel with people, especially people he had just met. And, the being never left his side.

Bill described a huge Christmas tree in the center of the town square that lit up the entire town. The amazing thing is that the tree had no lights on it, yet it lit up the entire place. He said he looked up to see the top of the tree, but it was so enormous and so high that it was impossible to see where it ended. He felt the tree represented the Lord because that tree provided the only source of light to the entire city, [and its presence was magnificent and commanding]. He asked the being if they took the tree down every year and the being told him, "No, it stays up all the time." Bill spoke of an amazing sense of love and peace such as he had never experienced here on earth. It was all around him and it radiated from the being, as well. He kept saying "It was amazing, Pris, absolutely amazing!"

Bill told me they came to an intersection where there were people in a church across the street. The music coming from the church was like nothing he had ever heard on earth. "It was the most beautiful music, Pris! I can't describe the sound. There is nothing on earth to compare it to, but it was so soothing and so beautiful!" He told me that people were singing the most beautiful songs as they went about their lives.

The being led him around the town, and they came to an area where there were cottages that people were living in. He said he could see what appeared to be families sitting at the dinner table eating, talking, and visibly enjoying being together. He told me he was very embarrassed by the question he asked the being at this point, and was actually quite perturbed that he did not ask a more profound question. When I pressed for what the question was, he said "How stupid! I asked if this is where Bob Cratchit lives! Can you believe that I'm with a heavenly being and, Pris... all I could think of to ask about is Bob Cratchit?" I smiled at the question and gave Bill a hug, knowing how much he loved those "Christmas Carol" movies.

Curiosity got the better of me, so I asked Bill what the being's response was to his question. He said, "He told me 'no, Bob lives on the other side of town. This is where *your* house is.' *My* house?" Bill asked. "Yes," the being said, "we are working on your house now, but it isn't ready yet. It will be ready soon, though, and you're really going to like it."

The being then led Bill to a street with different types of shops. Bill remembered that people were very welcoming and warm, waving to him and smiling as they walked by. They even waved at him from across the street. They acted as if they knew him, and he was surprised by that.

There was a bakery where the workers carried out baskets of different breads and shared them with others. Bill said people were not buying and selling but rather giving and taking. There was no exchange of money. "There was total peace and serenity, no stress what-so-ever!" he told me. The smell of ginger bread brought back memories of his mother who traditionally baked ginger bread cookies every Christmas. There was a meat store and he could smell an amazing aroma of goose coming from it. He told me his grandmother used to cook goose for Christmas dinner, not the traditional turkey. As they passed more stores, he said he could smell a strong aroma of sherry, which he said his father always enjoyed after dinner. He was awed by the experience, telling me, "I never liked sherry, but my father did." I was amazed at this part of the experience. I told him that I felt that his mother, father, and grandmother obviously knew he was coming and were waiting for him, but he could not see them yet because he had not been there to stay.

"Pris," he said, "I want to go back! I didn't want to wake up, and tonight when I go to sleep, I am going to try to go back. The peace and the love there were like nothing I can describe. They are far more intense than anything we feel here on earth." Then, he started to cry, and with tears flooding down his face, he held me and whispered, "When I go, and after you dry your tears, I want you to smile when you think of me in that amazing place. I was happy there, but I'll miss you terribly. So, when you get there, meet me in front of the bakery where I'll be waiting for you." He then expressed concern for me. "I am sorry I won't be here for you anymore. Who will take care of you?" I assured him that I would be fine. I told him that the kids would look after me, and that they would take good care of me.

"Pris," he said through his sobs, "I'll never stop loving you and I will miss you every second I'm there, so when you arrive, come right to the bakery! Okay?"

We held each other and cried for quite a while, and then I had to leave for work. Unfortunately, life's realities invade even those profound, heart-stopping moments. Well, the impact of this story was so intense, that I could not free myself from it. It completely consumed my thoughts and my emotions. I discussed it with two chaplains and several doctors I work with because I wanted both the spiritual and the medical opinion of what might have occurred. I wanted answers. I *needed* answers! The chaplains agreed that Bill had probably had an out-of-body experience, nearly dying. The doctors explained that Bill was accepting of his mortality and that it was a good thing that he was resigned to it. The one thing that everyone agreed on was the great amount of detail with which Bill described this experience. One chaplain told me she had heard many near-death stories but never had she heard one with such descriptive detail.

There is a lot in life I do not know. However, this one thing I do know—this vision/experience was a gift from God above! It freed Bill of severe depression, anxiety, and debilitating fear and gave him peace and hope, and the ability to throw his heart fully open to what life he had left. He went from being reclusive, dark, and edgy to being welcoming and loving in a way that he had not been able to do in a very long time. Bill set out to prepare all of us for what lay ahead. He left us with such an amazing gift of himself that none of us will ever be the same again. And, when I get lonely and miss him, I picture him in that city of peace and love and it comforts me and makes me smile, just as he wanted.

The Ending Draws Closer

After Bill's vision/experience, he was profoundly different. The depression lifted, he found his sense of wit again, and he opened his heart unabashedly to all. He was quick to forgive and to ask for forgiveness. In fact, he thought long and hard about people he might have hurt along the way, and he set out to apologize to each one. He would ask me to invite people to the house, which was very unusual because he had previously been so reclusive. In addition, people who came unexpectedly were whole-heartedly welcomed. The transformation was amazing!

Yes, Bill did still think about suicide sometimes, but it did not consume him as before. His promise to me was that he would not do that to the kids or to me. And, he kept that promise even though I know there were moments that were so difficult and so incredibly painful that he felt he could not go on another second longer. Instead of ending his life, he chose to reach out to God in those moments and to protect the life God had given him. I so admire him for that! For, his journey was SO hard, and the pain was getting much more intense as he watched, and felt, his body deteriorate. Bill always was spirited and fearless, but he took on a new level of bravery and courage. I was, and am, so proud of him for that! I did tell him that, too. I wanted him to know how much it meant to me that he faced death so heroically and with such a strong confidence and faith in God.

Bill set out to take care of his family and to prepare us for his death and our life afterwards. He would teach me how to do things for the house like wrapping the pipes for winter, and then add, "You will need to know this." I became the obedient student and he, the wise teacher. He answered all my questions, even the one I asked about what it felt like to be dying. He held nothing back. He made the absolute most of every second. He made every moment here count. Every word he spoke and everything he did was a deliberate act to give himself to us. He had conversations with each one of us—serious, from the bottom of his heart exchanges, so there would be no doubt about how much he loved us and how grateful he was to have each one of us in his life. He gave "heart" gifts of love and wisdom to each one of us. He also gave specific instructions to both Joe and Vicki about what each one would do for me following his death and in the years to come. He made absolutely sure that I was going to be cared for as meticulously as he had done for thirty-nine years.

Bill and I faced the inevitable with humor and grace. We talked about his death comfortably, and never treated it like the proverbial elephant in the room. When you have confidence in the validity of God's word, and you have embraced God's offer of salvation through Christ, you can face death with the assurance that you will see your loved one again. That is the wonderful hope we have in Christ. And, having that hope made it easier for Bill and me to face, head on, what would ultimately be the end of his natural life. We were at peace because we knew our separation was only temporary. We had the assurance that we would eventually see each other again, only the next time we met it would be for forever— in a place where we would never have to experience the depth of pain we were both experiencing! WOW!

One time, Vicki and I were having a conversation about what Bill would wear in his casket. Of course, I said "a suit." Vicki disagreed and thought he should wear what he loved most: shorts and a t-shirt. As fate would have it, Bill came hobbling down the hallway with his walker, and Vicki called to him, "Hey Dad, Mom and I are having a discussion about what we're going to dress you in when you die. Mom wants to put you in a suit but I think you should wear shorts and a t-shirt." He agreed with Vicki's choice, of course. Bill never did enjoy being in a suit and he really hated ties. He was truly most comfortable in shorts and a t-shirt, especially as he became more debilitated. However, we discussed it and everyone compromised. I agreed to no suit, and they agreed to slacks and a dress shirt. I won the argument about the tie, though! These types of dialogues took place as naturally as discussing what we were having for dinner. And, that gave us all the strength to face what lay ahead.

In January 2010, Bill was so sick that I had to put him on hospice. He required much more care than we could give him at home, but I just could not put him in a nursing home. I knew that Bill wanted to be at home with his family because we had discussed it. I also knew that he would not last long in a nursing home. When a friend suggested that I call hospice, I took her advice and made the call. I had never realized how much hospice helps in these situations, and I was so very grateful for the team who took care of Bill and encouraged me. They were a Godsend. They were so kind and supportive to both Bill and to me. Then, when Bill's death came, the entire team arrived at the house to support me. Several even came to his funeral. I also received a beautiful hand-written note from the volunteer who met with me several times to encourage me. Not only were they there during Bill's illness, but the grief counselor was there for me for thirteen months following his death. She called, visited, and checked up on me during those months. And I called her whenever I needed her help, which was quite often at first. She was always there for me. I will never get over that!

A Strong, Supportive Family

*V*icki was very open and honest with the girls about what was happening to Bill. She always welcomed their questions and answered each one in a patient, loving manner. Since she is a nurse, she could also provide a knowledgeable explanation to them. There were no secrets. We all knew what was happening, even the girls. We all laughed and we all cried, and we were all there for each other. We are a family, and we were wonderfully strong together.

Although Tina was the youngest grandchild, she was the most deeply connected to Bill. She suffered greatly as she watched him decline but she could not really express what she was feeling, until one day she found the words. She went to Vicki and told her, "Mommy, my heart fills with tears for my Buddy then they come out my eyes when I cry." My four-year-old granddaughter had discovered an amazingly profound way to describe her broken heart. Oh, how much she loved her Buddy! And, oh, how deeply she was hurting!

One evening in mid-March 2010 about six weeks before Bill died, Vicki felt the time was right to talk to the girls about Bill's decline and his inevitable death. She took them into her bedroom and told them that Poppy was going to go to Heaven soon. Though we did not know the exact time, it was definitely going to happen. The girls cried, and had a lot of questions. Questions like, what will it be like? When will it happen? What will Poppy look like when he is dead? Vicki answered all of their questions telling them that Poppy would continue to get weaker and more tired. Eventually, he would sleep a lot and then he would just stop breathing. When that happened, he would change color and we would know that he was gone. Tina was especially interested in hearing about Heaven since her Buddy was going to go there, and Vicki had a chance to explain how, when we love Jesus, we can go to Heaven when we die. Tina, whose thinking processes are always in high gear, asked her mother, "Is Nanny going to go to Heaven?" Vicki answered, "Yes." Then she asked if Vicki was going to go to Heaven and the answer was, "Yes." Tina proceeded to name every person in the family, asking if each one would be in Heaven, and after there was no one left to ask about, she said, "Oh no! I'll be all alone!" Even in the midst of great sorrow, Tina has a gift for bringing laughter! After comforting the girls, they all finally went to bed. I greatly admire the way Vicki handled this situation with the girls. Our natural tendency is to shield children from the pain of life. However, Vicki's belief is that pain is a part of life, and that children should be taught how to face and manage that pain. Shielding them is not helpful to them. Besides, they know that *something* is going on, and not to include them is much more frightening to them. The girls accepted the situation with such amazing grace and love. And, they all taught me a huge lesson about facing life's pain together, as well.

The next morning, Bill was sitting in his wheelchair in the living room and Tina joined him. She crawled onto his lap and said, "Hi Buddy." Bill replied with "Hi Little Buddy." This was their daily routine. The routine, however, quickly took a sharp turn south when she looked up at him and announced in a full, loud voice, "So, I hear you're going to be dead!" When Bill called me and told this to me, he said, "Pris, it took my breath away! And, I don't have very much to begin with!" I realized at that point that no one had told Bill about the conversation Vicki had had with the girls the night before, which I then mentioned to him. Then, I asked Bill what he said to her, and he said he told her that, yes, he was going to die. He was going to go to Heaven to be with Grandma, who had died just two months before, and they were going to hold hands and walk around Heaven and see all the beautiful sights together. He told her that he would wait for all of us to get there—one by one—and that he would be there to meet each one of us when our turn came. But when *her* turn came, he would be right in front because she was his Little Buddy! Tina replied with, "OK," and she got down from his lap and went to her room to play. Oh, the amazing resilience kids have!

That evening when I returned home from work, I sat down in my usual place on the couch. Ashlyn came over to me, gave me a big hug, and we clung to each other for the longest time. There was no need for words. Sometimes, a hug says it all, and that was one of those moments. When Ashlyn left, Samantha came over. She asked me, "Is Poppy going to look fake like Grandma?" She was referring to the way my mother looked in her casket. I told her, "Yes, he is." Samantha and I hugged, also. No further dialogue was required. Finally, Tina came over to me. She sat in my lap, and I held her tightly as she told me, "When my Buddy dies, Nanny, I won't watch Sponge Bob anymore."

I mentioned that statement to Bill, and asked him to talk to Tina because she needed his help handling her life after his death. At the right moment, Bill talked to Tina. He told her that when he died, he wanted her to keep watching Sponge Bob. He said he would be watching her from Heaven, and it would make him very happy to know that she was still enjoying Sponge Bob even though he couldn't physically be with her. Bill told Tina that seeing her watch Sponge Bob would make him smile, and she promised him that she would do that. Yes, Bill knew that scripture does not indicate whether people who have gone to Heaven can see us, but this was his way of comforting Tina and helping her to handle her grief. He loved her so much, and it deeply hurt his heart knowing the pain his death was going to cause her.

Being so open and honest with the girls put us all at ease with the situation, and gave us many opportunities to support each other. We all took our turns crying during this ordeal. And when it was each one's turn to cry, the rest of us were there with lots of hugs and kisses. We were all the givers and recipients of the love and support. It was amazing seeing the strength of those little ones, as well as how much they actually understood about what was happening.

There were many special moments for me during this time. As painful as this situation was for me, and as much of a toll as it was taking on me, I had many wonderful conversations with Bill, Joe, Vicki, and the girls. Many Saturday mornings I would rise early because I just could not sleep and I would go to the living room to sit quietly to try to sort out my thoughts. Life was so overwhelming at this point that I had to keep my fear in check by having every detail in order in my mind or I felt that I would completely fall apart. On many of those mornings, Vicki joined me and we had a chance to share our fears, talk about what we were observing in Bill's decline, and discuss what the road ahead might hold for all of us. While everyone else was asleep, and in the quietness and peace of the early morning, Vicki and I cried together, laughed together, strategized a new plan together, and gave each other strength. I will always cherish those exchanges and the special connection I share with my wonderful daughter.

The months that followed were both painful and joyful at the same time. We watched Bill continue his decline, but we enjoyed having him emotionally back with us again. Bill talked to me about everything—his fears, his regrets, his joys, and his triumphs. We tied up all the loose ends, and reconciled anything that had been even a tiny issue. We left nothing unsaid or unfelt. Our hearts were one, and it was both cleansing and healing. That was such a special gift for us. And, although we never actually discussed it, we both knew that this was all part of the letting go to the ultimate, concluding moment when it was all over. I learned that letting go is a process that takes place moment by moment, tear by tear, and smile by smile until the final good-bye. As painful as that was, it was also a very precious phase in our journey. We cried, we laughed, sometimes we laughed through our tears, and at times, we cried through our laughter.

Bill still wanted to go, but he wanted to stay, too. He was in such conflict! He talked about fighting to stay so he could at least see his granddaughters graduate from high school though he said he didn't think he'd be able to stay long enough to see Tina graduate because she was only four. I secretly didn't think that it was even remotely possible that he would be here for another eight to ten years, but the thought gave him hope and I was very happy for that.

Spiritual Strength

The most amazing thing occurred to Bill during this journey. I noticed that as Bill's physical man weakened, his spiritual man strengthened. He read his Bible every day as he sat in his wheelchair, a habit that he had lost along the way but now had found again. While he read his Bible, his Little Buddy always sat on the couch next to his wheelchair with her little pink children's New Testament. He enjoyed watching her pretending to read. And she never turned a page until he turned one in his Bible. He smiled when he told that to me for those moments gave him such great joy! Tina and Bill continued this ritual until his eyes failed him and he could no longer read or understand the words on the page. Both Bibles were left in their usual place on the table next to Bill's wheelchair—with her small pink New Testament on top of his large-print NIV version—until he died, at which time they were tucked away for safe keeping. At some point in her future, Tina will have that little pink New Testament again. And on the front page of it, she will find a hand-written note from her Buddy that he wrote to her just a few weeks before he died.

Amazing Love

God had given Bill, me, and our family a wonderful gift of love. A strong love had been at the very core of our relationship even through the difficult times. But, during the months following his vision/experience, Bill totally opened his heart to me as he had not been able to do in a very long time. And, my heart responded. I was so happy! I did not think a person could feel such heights of joy and depths of pain at the same time, but I did. It was as if Bill and I fell in love all over again, and that was such a great treasure for both of us. I even told him once, "I finally got the man I've always wanted, and you're going to leave me." He smiled and said, "Yeah, isn't that something."

Everyone felt the love in our home. God had filled every nook and cranny with it. Bill's caretaker commented on it, and the hospice people noticed it. Friends that visited mentioned it, and we all reveled in it. It was amazing!

The End

About a month or so before he died, Bill asked to see Jimmie. He said he was grateful to Jimmie for arranging our blind date because he could not have asked for a better, more loving, supportive wife. So, I called Jimmie and we made plans for him to come for a visit. He was to arrive on Saturday, April 24th and planned to leave on Monday, April 26th. I could not wait for his visit because I knew it meant a lot to Bill.

Bill kept getting worse, and I knew he could not go on much longer. He was sleeping much more and getting visibly weaker every day. His dementia was getting worse, and he was losing his eyesight and hearing. He had long since given up reading because his brain could not process the words. He was eating less and slowly getting more distant from us. We could see it and he said he could feel it. I will be forever grateful to the pathologists I work with, for when the doctors hesitated to give me the information I sought, the pathologists gave it to me straight. Nothing was ever sugar coated. They answered all my questions candidly, yet gently. They will never know how much I appreciate that because it not only helped me to plan for the inevitable, but it helped me to brace myself for what lay ahead. I greatly respect them for their honesty. It was just what I needed to be able to keep myself together by knowing how to manage each development in the situation. And, I not only had to manage events in my personal life, but in my professional life, as well. Having the pathologists to talk "real" to was invaluable as I juggled all my responsibilities while trying to be there with, and for, Bill.

On April 15th, Bill was put on morphine by the hospice doctor. And, with the advice of the pathologists I work with, I took a leave of absence. As of April 16th, I was home full-time. Bill was so happy to have me home with him! He loved having me there all the time because he did not want to die alone. And, my near presence was a great comfort to Bill. He was totally reliant on me to take care of him and he needed me to make the appropriate medical decisions on his behalf and in accordance with his wishes. I prudently and respectfully took on that responsibility.

On Wednesday, April 21st, Bill asked me, "Pris, have I left anything undone?" I really did not want to answer his question because I knew it meant he was ready to go and I did not want to give him the okay to do so. I was not ready yet to give him an official release. However, our pact of honesty won over and after a slight hesitation, I gave him the answer. "No, Bill, you've taken care of everything. You are just waiting to see Jimmie." He asked me when Jimmie was arriving, and I told him, "A few more days." Bill sighed so tiredly and whispered, "Okay," then fell asleep. He was sleeping a lot at that point, but it was a more peaceful sleep because he knew I was always near at hand.

We got through the next few days, and the morphine was a huge help with Bill's pain. I was grateful for that. Because of the peripheral arterial disease, his legs were literally decaying from the inside out and we had to treat them with special wound care medication and wraps. They oozed constantly and caused him such horrible discomfort. In addition, we had all kinds of medical equipment in the house, and Bill was tethered to an oxygen tank. It was heart wrenching! However, we were glad to be together, and we made the most of every day.

The morning of April 24th, Bill was lying in bed, and when he awoke I told him, "Bill, Jimmie will be here today." "Today? Is he here now?" Bill asked excitedly. "No, Bill, he isn't here yet, but I'm leaving at noon to get him from the airport," I replied.

The weekend with Jimmie could not have been more perfect! I had invited my siblings and their spouses to be with us, Joe and Vicki and their families were at the house, and friends stopped by all weekend. It was as if God prompted them to see Bill one more time before he left, and they came and we all enjoyed. Bill and Jimmie reminisced about their school days together and some of their antics that caused them problems with the principal. Others met and got to know each other, and our home was filled with love and laughter. It was one of the most amazing weekends of my life! Bill was so tired and weak, but he would not lie down. He insisted on sitting in his wheelchair and being with everyone. I was worried about him, and I kept telling him he needed to lie down because I wanted him to be comfortable. But he very patiently said, "I want to be here with everyone. Please, Pris." So I backed off, and even though he kept falling asleep in the wheelchair and I was afraid he would fall out, I let him stay with us. I just constantly kept an eye on him to be sure he was safe. For a brief moment in all the horror we had been living with for so long, I was really enjoying myself. It was good to see our friends, and great to have Jimmie and our family here. The love was palpable. I will always cherish that weekend!

Monday arrived and Jimmie got ready to leave. He and Bill hugged before Jimmie left for the airport. Bill was happy to have seen him again. It had been way too long...

Right after Jimmie left, two more friends stopped by and Bill enjoyed his visit with both of them. He was SO tired, and he did have to lie down. However, he had a wonderful visit with our friend, Vera, and he was so happy she was able to stop by. Bill always loved Vera. She is one of those people who fills a room with love just by entering it. You can feel it. And, Vera has more challenges than you can ever imagine. But she absolutely, totally loves God and everyone she meets! She has been an inspiration to Bill and me since I first met her in 1995 when I started working at the hospital. In fact, many times when Bill felt he couldn't handle things any longer, I would remind him of everything Vera deals with. And how, by relying fully on God and keeping focused on Him, she has been able to overcome some insurmountable health issues—and for a very long time. Those reminders helped him immensely and gave him the strength to deal with his own situation.

There was a definite change in Bill, and the hospice nurse told me he probably did not have more than a week left. The pain I felt in my heart was so intense that it was a physical pain. I just did not think I could do this, and I came to understand the enormity of the term *broken heart*. I felt like I was going to have a heart attack, the heaviness and pain in my chest were so great. I prayed for God to hold that off until this was over. I needed to be with Bill every second we had left. I had promised him years before when this whole journey began that I would walk this road with him—side by side — until the very end and that he would not walk it alone. I was absolutely determined to keep that promise.

Monday evening was a nightmare! Bill's kidneys had started to shut down, and he was crazed and restless. And, he was definitely not in his right mind. I could not get him into bed, and was up with him the entire night. He did not know what he was saying or doing. He became a person I did not know. He was argumentative and difficult. He was not *my* Bill—the Bill who, in thirty-nine years, never raised his voice to me. Finally, at about 6:00 Tuesday morning, he let me put him into bed. I called hospice and they sent a nurse to check on him. Again, it was determined that Bill would probably be gone by Friday or Saturday.

I called Joe at work, and asked him to come home because his Dad was not doing well, and we needed him at the house. Joe arrived within ten minutes, and he never left. Vicki also called her job to let them know she would not be in. The three of us did what we could to keep Bill safe and comfortable, checking on him every few minutes.

By Tuesday afternoon, Bill had started to slip into a coma. I sat on the bed next to him with my laptop and wrote the different parts of the funeral program as he rested. I could not leave him. I had to be with him. Bill was in and out of consciousness, and the kids checked on him often. Little did I know that when I put him into bed that morning, he would never leave it again alive.

That night, I crawled into bed completely exhausted—physically, mentally, and emotionally. I was totally depleted. There was nothing left. In fact, I felt as if I was in the red zone on the physical and emotional scales. It is unbelievably difficult to describe the heaviness of the burden and the depth of the pain you feel knowing your spouse of thirty-nine years has only a day or two to be with you. There are just no words! As I had always done every night before, I placed my head on Bill's shoulder and ended the day with, "I love you." I didn't expect to hear from him because he hadn't spoken all day, though every time I had told him, "I love you, Bill" he did try to respond. Well, to my great and wonderful surprise, he whispered in a tiny, barely audible breath, "I love you." Those were the last words we ever spoke to each other.

On Wednesday, April 28th, 2010, at 1:00 p.m., Bill went to be with the Lord—a mere 48 hours after he completed the last thing on his list—to see Jimmie, and ten months—to the day—after his vision/experience. And, he went as he wished—at home in his own bed—with his son, his daughter, his Little Buddy (who was only four years old), and me there with him.

As Bill took his journey I couldn't help but think about the place where he was going—the place of unimaginable peace and love—to be with his family and all the others who had gone on before him. I thought how amazing it was that he would be in the very presence of the Lord, Himself! What a moment that was! Bill had arrived safely home, and that thought brought great comfort to me.

Just moments after Bill died Vicki realized that Tina was no longer in the room. She went through the house to look for Tina, and found her in her bedroom watching TV. Vicki asked Tina what she was doing, and she told her mother that she was watching Sponge Bob "'Cause my Buddy said when he died, I had to watch Sponge Bob." Oh, how pure and literal the little ones are!

Dear Friends

ou know, God has such an amazing plan for all of us if we would just trust Him with our lives. He knows what we will need long before we even realize we will need it. If we trust Him to take care of us, He does exactly that. There is no road we walk but that He hasn't been there before us and planned for our needs. There are no coincidences when you trust God. Those moments are His way of loving and caring for us. There is order to each event, encounter, and experience in our lives. He is so awesome, and I love Him so very much!

Back in 1980, we had met a couple, John and Janet Willis, in a church we attended in Houston. We became very close friends, but through the years, we had lost touch. Then, quite unexpectedly, I ran into Janet in a church in Katy that I had started to attend. What a reunion that was! And, we were all reconnected again. It was just that simple. It was so good to have John and Janet back in our lives. Both Bill and I really enjoyed being with them again. They were understanding and accepting of Bill's depression and reclusiveness, and being with them was so easy. It was a wonderful re-friendship, just as the original friendship had been earlier.

John was one of the two people who had stopped by the house after Jimmie left. He and Bill had sat in the living room and had eaten Blue Bell together, enjoying a wonderful visit. Bill had become very tired, and after I put him back into bed, John and I chatted for a while.

51

When John left, he said, "Pris, if you need anything—*anything*—you call me. Any time…you call me!" I knew he meant it!

At the moment that Bill died, I needed Janet. I do not know why you need any specific person at any particular moment in time, but I absolutely had to have Janet with me. I called John and told him that Bill had died, and that I needed Janet. I was crying very hard, and John said he would call her "right now." Time is a blur, but it was not long before Janet arrived. A little while later, John came, too. I drew strength just having them in my home with me.

I held up pretty well until the two men from the funeral home arrived to take Bill. Suddenly, I was completely panic-stricken. I don't know why but I just hadn't thought about this. I hadn't even considered the fact that Bill would be taken away. The thought of Bill not in our home with me was one that my brain could not—would not—accept! I needed more time with him. My brain felt like it was spinning out of control. Every emotion I could possibly feel was filling my being all at the same time. I did not know what to do with all those feelings and I wanted to jump out of my skin. I absolutely could not let them take Bill. I was not ready yet! It was way too soon! I asked if I could have just a minute with Bill, and they graciously agreed. I knew I was detaining them, but I truly did not care. This was very out of character for me because I am the kind of person who always thinks of others first. However, this was *my* time with *my* husband, and I was going to have it! I did not even feel bad about making my own needs the priority.

I went back into the bedroom and that was it— the dam broke! I threw myself across Bill's body, held on to him with everything in me, and completely fell apart. Oh, I knew Bill was gone. But there was something comforting about having his body still with us. And, I just couldn't bear the thought of him leaving our home and never, ever coming back again. That was far more than I could handle. All the anxiety, strain, exhaustion, and fears I had been holding in for the last several years swept over me like a tidal wave. I sobbed from a place deep, deep within me, and I could not stop. I clung desperately to Bill. I never wanted to let him go. I was inconsolable. My heart was shattered and I was completely depleted. I absolutely could not have them take my Bill. I just could not do it! This was one of the most profoundly, utterly devastating moments of my entire life.

Everyone gave me my time with Bill. However, after a few minutes, Janet and John came into the room. Joe and Vicki followed, and they all tried very hard to help me. I just could not respond. I felt paralyzed by my grief. It was overwhelming and more intensely painful than words can ever describe. It robbed me of my strength and my legs felt like rubber. I felt like I would fall if I stood up. I had pain in my chest and I could not breathe. Janet asked John to pray for me. I do not remember what he said, but I know his prayer brought me peace. And with gentle, but firm coaxing, I was able to free my hold of Bill and leave the room.

As word got out, people started coming to the house. I remember a lot of talking, and I remember having to answer many questions from the hospice people. However, I cannot tell you who was there or what I was doing. And, the entire time, people shielded me from seeing Bill's body being taken out of the house.

You know, we can learn something every single day, even in the midst of the most horrendous situations. And, that day I learned a very valuable lesson. For, while all the "busyness" was going on, Janet was stripping my bed, washing the bedding, and putting the bed all back together again. I never realized how important a practical act of kindness could mean to someone who is in such deep despair. At some point, I became too exhausted to function, and I went to my room to lie down. What a gift had been given to me—the gift of freshly cleaned bedding! It welcomed me with comforting open "arms" and I collapsed into a deep sleep, thankful for my dear friend's huge, practical act of kindness.

I have heard the story of Mary and Martha from the Bible preached many times. And somehow Mary, the friend of Jesus who chose to sit at His feet and visit with Him, was always portrayed as having made the better choice than her sister, Martha, who prepared food and refreshments for Jesus and their visitors. And, I do get that! But, I learned that day how much we also need the Martha's of this world. They provide real, practical help. And they seem to know innately the perfect thing to do and at just the right time, as well. When you are in as great a need as I was at that point, the "Martha's" are the people who take care of you. Janet was my "Martha" that day. I am forever grateful!

The Funeral

The only thing I remember during the several days before the funeral is going to the funeral home and settling all the details of the initial arrangements we had made before Bill died. The kids and I also shopped for clothes for Bill. I know a lot of people stopped by the house, but I can't tell you who they were. I think I slept a lot on-and-off, but I do not remember. I was in a completely dazed frame of mind. My brain was completely shut down and I was on autopilot. I know that every time I came out of my room there was more food, and it started to overtake my dining room and kitchen. We even had "tons" of paper plates, cups, plastic utensils, and soft drinks that filled my utility room. I was amazed at the outpouring of love—practical love, again—from our friends, coworkers, neighbors, and Vicki's church. I do not know if I thanked everyone for their generosity. If I have not thanked you, and you are one of those "angels" reading this book, you will never know how much your act of kindness meant to my family and me. Thank you!

Monday, May 3, 2010 was the day of Bill's funeral. I thought I was holding up fairly well as I got ready, and I was proud of that. I kept telling myself that I was, after all, a strong woman and that I could face this. With God's help (and believe me, I was relying on it!) I could get through the day. When I arrived at the funeral home, however, I felt all my strength drain from me. Grief swept over me, I could hardly breathe, and I knew I couldn't do it. I just could not face this. I started to cry. I found a chair and sat down, but I so desperately wanted to lay my head on Bill's shoulder and tell him how much I love him one last time. So, I got up and walked to his casket. The closest I could get to his shoulder was to lay my head on the corner of his casket by his head. When I did that, the floodgates opened again, and I could not stop sobbing. My daughter and son came up to me and tried to comfort me, but there was no comfort. There was just incapacitating pain. I just couldn't think of not seeing my dear husband ever again. It was more than my heart, my emotions, my brain, and my body could bear. How do you say, "Good-bye" for the last time to someone who has been a part of your entire adult life—and such an important, intimate part? I had never had to do that before. My brain kept screaming at me, *I don't know how to do this! I don't know how to do this! How can I do something no one's ever taught me how to do?"* How do I do this? My sobbing continued, and that physical heaviness and pain in my chest became more intense.

Vicki and Joe finally got me to agree to go into the next room where they sat me down in one of the comfortable chairs there. Janet also came over to that room, and she got me a glass of water. They all talked to me to calm me down, but I don't know what they said. I remember that someone came over and coaxed me into taking a little pill that would "help me get through the funeral." I did not want to take that medication, but I truly had no choice. The funeral would never be able to progress as long as I was in that hysterical state. In addition, we had a designated time that we absolutely had to be at the cemetery, so I finally agreed.

I remember very little about the funeral service. But, I do know that it was a beautiful celebration of Bill's life and our children's eulogies were awesome! Joe told stories about Bill's wonderful sense of humor and the practical jokes Bill had played on him through the years while Vicki focused on Bill's loving, caring heart. I remember how bravely and confidently they spoke of their father's life. They were absolutely amazing! I could not have felt more proud of them.

And, I could not believe that I had been given the privilege of being their mother. I felt so blessed, and I was so very grateful. We are a strong family, and that was clearly visible to all. Following the service, I received many comments about how wonderful Bill's funeral was, what a great celebration of his life it was, and how superbly my children had handled themselves. People commented on how lovingly Joe and Vicki took care of me while in the midst of their own personal grief. Even the funeral director told me, "Your children did their father proud. And, they took such good care of you. You don't see that very often, Priscilla. You have two wonderful kids." He wasn't telling me something I didn't already know and that I am not acutely aware of every second of my life! I wanted Bill to have a perfect memorial, and he absolutely did. It had been flawless.

Following the funeral, we went to the Houston National Cemetery where Bill was given a full military funeral with honors. I had seen that on TV and in movies, but had never witnessed it in person. It was very moving and emotional, and I felt so proud of Bill and his voluntary service to our country. Bill had been very proud to serve in the Navy back in the late sixties, and he willingly went to Viet Nam in support of America, volunteering to do so. And, though he never enjoyed being the center of attention, this was all *about* him and *for* him. I had told him we were going to give him a full military funeral with the American flag draping his casket and a 21-gun salute, and he was very moved by that. He smiled and thanked me for doing that for him. Bill never expected much from life. He was a simple man. All he ever needed was his children, his grandchildren, and me. So, having this particular honor bestowed on him was very special to him, and I am glad I was able to do it.

After the graveside service was complete, I headed towards the car. I was beyond exhausted in every way imaginable, and I just wanted to get through the rest of the day. However, there was one more thing we had to do, and it was at Bill's specific request. Margaret, Bill's caretaker, came up to me with a handful of balloons in various colors.

She told me that before he had died, Bill had given her money and asked her to buy a balloon for each member of our family. He had named each person and had told her what color balloon each person was to receive. She said he wanted all of us to let the balloons go at the same time. I told her I just couldn't do that because I was simply too tired. But she held a white balloon out to me telling me Bill specifically asked her to buy a white one for his bride. I had no choice but to comply. It was his last wish. Margaret explained to us that Bill had told her that when we saw all the balloons soaring to the sky, we would know that his spirit was free. And, I have to tell you, that was a most healing moment for me. How did Bill know that by seeing those balloons heading towards the heavens, I would actually be able to know—really know—that he was completely free? It was just the perfect ending to the graveside ceremony. Bill was still taking care of me after all, and I really needed it! A friend of mine took pictures of the soaring balloons. It was a glorious moment.

We returned to the funeral home where my sister-in-law, Debbie, had arranged for an Italian feast for all our guests and us. This particular funeral home has a wonderful reception room with "cushy" sofas and comfortable chairs, beautiful artwork and artifacts, and the perfect place for receiving guests. As part of the funeral costs, we were offered the use of that beautiful room for our reception. Since food pervades all facets of an Italian's life (I am of Italian descent), and a funeral is no exception, I was pleased to have the room to visit with everyone who took time from their busy life to honor Bill and to support me. It was a wonderful feast of different pastas, meats, salad, and garlic bread. Following the meal, we had dessert—enough dessert to feed nearly the entire city of Houston! Yes, this *is* an exaggeration, but you now have an image of the number of desserts we had. And, in true "Martha" style, all those desserts were a gift from the women at Vicki's church. What a wonderful message those desserts gave—the message that, "although I don't know you, I can still love you and care for you." I felt treasured by people I did not even know. What an amazing blessing!

We had one more rite of passage to accomplish before we were done. We had to have Blue Bell ice cream. How could we send Bill on to his reward without having Blue Bell in his honor? So, at my request, Debbie provided a Blue Bell ice cream cup for each one of us. It was a wonderful moment as we all held our cups up and said, "To Bill!" When we started to eat the ice cream, however, it was as hard as a rock. Debbie had stored it in dry ice, and it was frozen solid. We had to hold our cups up to the light bulbs in the lamps to soften the ice cream enough so we could even *begin* to eat it. We all had a good laugh, and I know that had Bill been there, he would have really enjoyed the moment. I am sure he would have had something witty to say that would have made us laugh even harder. He *was* quiet and he *was* always most comfortable in the background, but he loved to be the cause of our hysterical laughter. I felt that this was one last hearty laugh for the road, and that that was befitting to Bill. I always smile when I think of that moment, because Bill had told everyone before he died that if they owned any stock in Blue Bell, they had better sell it. He assured them that when he was gone, the stock would plummet. His addiction was so well known, that several of the floral arrangements at his funeral were in Blue Bell containers. Those containers were real conversation pieces to visitors who were not aware of how much he loved that ice cream.

Time to Grieve

Finally, it was time to go home. Joe was a huge help in getting all the flowers and plants into his truck and taking them home to me. He handled all the details at the funeral, greeted visitors, and made sure everything went as planned. He was absolutely wonderful and I needed his help more than he can ever know. In their own roles, both my children took care of me both directly and indirectly. And, I know that even in the midst of their own personal grief, their eyes were on me making sure that I was doing well. It just doesn't get any better than that!

As I walked out of the funeral home, the words of a friend kept running through my mind: "You take care of yourself, Priscilla, because grieving is hard work." Little did I know just how hard that journey was going to be!

———————————— ⨍ ————————————

Days Following the Funeral

$\mathcal{J}$ remember very little of the days following the funeral. I know that I had told Bill before he died that when all was said and done, I had planned to drive to New York to see my family there. Not only do I find driving therapeutic, but my older sister, Jessie (we call her "Jess") is one of those individuals who loves to take care of people. She enjoys cooking your favorite foods and showering you with lots of hugs and love. And, I knew I would need all the tender loving care she would happily pour on me. Bill had told me, "Do what you need to do, Pris. Just be careful and please be safe."

I had planned to leave for New York by myself on May 15, just two-and-a-half weeks after Bill's death. No one could talk me out of that trip even though everyone told me they were concerned for my safety. I kept insisting that the road trip would do me good and that I would be fine. About a week after Bill died, I visited my doctor because I just could not sleep. When I told him about my trip, he insisted that I take a friend with me. I apparently have a stubborn streak in me because I told him the same thing I'd been telling everyone else—I said I would be fine. However, the concerned look on his face when I left the office made me wonder if, in fact, I was doing the right thing. A few days later, a very dear friend of mine gave me the same advice. "Pris," she said, "Don't go alone. You have no idea how low your emotions can sink when you are alone. You will not be able to concentrate on the road, and you will put yourself and others at risk. Please ask someone to go with you."

Well, I may be stubborn, but I am also smart, and hearing the same message from two different sources who do not know each other, made me think that I should heed their advice. Besides, I knew I was not myself and I had never driven cross-country before. Reason told me that this was not the time to start! So, I called my friend, Janet, and asked her, "How'd you like to go to New York?"

"Giiiirrrlll," she said, "I am there!" Her reaction absolutely made my day, and we proceeded to plan our trip for mid-May.

The morning of Saturday, May 15, 2010, with bags packed and the gas tank filled, I was ready to leave. However, as I walked out the door, I found that I did not want to go. I felt as if I was leaving Bill behind, and I just could not do that. I went back into the house, stood in my bedroom looking around the room. As I walked back to the living room, I started to cry. I cried hard—sobbed, in fact. I felt like I was walking out on Bill, and that I would lose the feeling of his presence in the house if I left. The feeling was so strong, in fact, that if I had not promised Janet this trip, I would have canceled it. So, I talked to Bill. I told him that I was leaving for New York as we had agreed, that I really needed this trip, and that I would be back. I asked him to wait for me to return. I told him I loved him and walked out the door, tears flowing down my face.

On The Way

I stopped at Janet's house and we put her luggage in the car. Janet got into the front passenger seat and we backed out of the driveway heading towards New York. It was raining torrentially, and I really didn't feel like being out in such a bad storm. Nevertheless, off we went with my GPS, my iPod with my favorite gospel music, and my dear friend with me!

I do not remember very much about the trip except that we had hammering rains the entire way from Texas to New York. We could only drive during daylight because we simply could not see at all during the evening. So, we just took our time and enjoyed what we could of the journey. We could not do much sightseeing along the way because every time we got out of the car, we got soaked. We looked like two drowned rats, we had really bad hairdos, and the novelty of that wore off very quickly. However, it was what it was and we made the best of it.

I do know that I cried on and off during the trip, and Janet was the perfect friend. She let me talk, cry, reminisce, and mourn without offering any advice or preventing me from doing so. We talked and shared from our hearts, and even enjoyed some good laughs along the way.

Janet and I are both huge fans of the Gaither Vocal Band, so we were happy to be able to listen to as much of their music as we wanted. We sang along and sometimes just listened. That music, God's presence, and Janet's support were what sustained me. She just seemed to know the perfect thing to say or to do at just the right moment. And the trip was a wonderful journey of faith, friendship, fun, and fascinating sights through the rain-soaked windshield.

It took us three days to arrive in New York and it was a wonderful moment when I pulled into the driveway of my sister's house, the rain still pouring down. We got out of the car and walked towards the front door but I entered the house apprehensively. I hadn't seen this part of my family in several years. And, though I was very happy to be with them again, I just didn't know how I would react seeing them after everything I had just experienced.

The Visit Begins

I remember walking through the doorway and Jess was the first person to greet me. We hugged tightly and she told me how glad she was to see me, how sorry she was, and how much she loved me. Next, came my brother-in-law, Charlie, who kissed me hello, hugged me, and said, "Hi, Pris" with such tenderness in his voice and incredible sadness in his eyes. I remember walking over to my nephew, Steve, next and that's when the tears came. He held me tightly and told me he was very sorry as I sobbed in his arms. He was so sweet and so comforting, and I could see such sorrow in his eyes at my plight.

When I moved away from Steve, his wife, Adrienne, was there to greet me also telling me how sorry she was. My niece, Debbie, was next, and then her husband, Joe. Everyone was so loving and so kind, and their tears in sharing my pain meant more to me than they will ever know. I knew at that moment, that I had made the right decision and that I was exactly where I needed to be if I was going to recover from my broken heart.

When I dried my eyes and pulled myself together, I realized that Janet was already meeting my family. That is just how my family is—they welcome everyone into their home and their hearts. They do not need formal introductions and you do not have to prove your worthiness. You just enter their home and you are part of the "gang." There just is not a better, more loving, forgiving, supportive family than mine, and I am so blessed to be a part of it. So many people are at odds with their siblings, but my two sisters, brother, and I have always maintained a warm, loving, supportive relationship with each other. Yes, we have had our moments, but they were just blips on the screen of life. We are all so different from each other, and that can obviously bring differences of opinion. However, we have always been able to appreciate each other's strengths and forgive our weaknesses. And, we have always been there for each other, especially through the rough spots. It just does not get any better than that! I love my siblings dearly. …always will!

My sister had dinner ready for us and we sat down to eat. Jess prayed and thanked God for giving Janet and me a safe journey, asking Him to be near me in a very special way and to surround me with His love and comfort. Those words were very soothing to me. As I sat there physically, emotionally, and mentally exhausted with my heart shattered in a million pieces, I welcomed those words with everything in me.

It is such a huge blessing to have others pray for us when we are too devastated to pray for ourselves. That is an amazing gift! Scripture tells us to pray for each other in James 5:16 (NIV) because "the prayer of a righteous man is powerful and effective." I can attest to that!

Deep Mourning Begins

I spent two weeks with my family in New York. It is difficult for me to remember everything we did and all the people we saw, but a few special moments do stand out in my mind. The entire time I spent there was very surreal. I know I was there. I know I talked, I smiled, and I cried. However, it did not feel real. I was on autopilot and going through the motions of being okay, but I could not have been farther from okay if I tried. I remember being completely exhausted. I could not get enough sleep. The smallest, most routine task was more overwhelming and exhausting than I can put into words. I felt as if I would drop to the floor if I tried to do too much, which was pretty much *anything*. Taking a shower took all the strength and energy I could muster, and I found myself walking away from conversations and gatherings to go lie down and sleep. I could not concentrate, and was easily annoyed by the normal chatter of life. I did not want to be with anyone, yet I *needed* to be with them. It was all so very bizarre!

Fear, darkness, and pain were my new companions. But by being with my family, they were at least manageable. I did not like the emotional place where I was. It was not who I am. I am all about being happy, positive, and enjoying life, even during the difficult times. Nevertheless, life had put me here and I had no choice but to walk this road. There was no getting off it, no detours around it, and no tunnels under it. There was only one way above it—my faith in

Jesus Christ. And, I held on to that faith, and Him, as I'd never done before. I embraced that faith tighter than I ever had in my entire life. I clung to it as strongly as I could, knowing that it was the one thing that I needed more than anything else if I was going to come back from this hideous place. Sometimes it is not about what you want or don't want, what you think you can handle or not handle, or what you feel strong enough to manage or not manage. Sometimes it is simply all about what life hands you. Those are very hard places to be in, and even more profoundly difficult to come back from.

I remember wanting to come out of this place—this dark, cold, painful, fearful valley—to be normal again. However, I discovered that I could not go back to what had been normal since it was forever gone. I really struggled with that because everything had changed and I had done nothing to cause that change. In fact, I did everything I could to keep Bill here with me. Nevertheless, I had no control over what had happened, so I had no choice but to accept my situation and to do what I had to, to get my life back again. I thought about that all the time and I finally came to realize that I would have to create a new normal. But, I didn't know how to do that. How do you come back from such a devastating place? How do you rebuild your life when everything is in ruins at your feet and you do not have the strength even to get out of bed or to take a shower? I did not know and I desperately wanted to know! I wanted answers. I *needed* answers! I needed help!

God`s Blessings Come in Nuggets of Pure Gold

*T*here are several people in New York who were angels sent
from Heaven above to minister to my broken heart. I learned
that it doesn't always take a long, profound sermon; a lengthy, pious
prayer; or a loud, powerful oration to touch your heart—especially if
the message is from God. You see, God speaks in whispers, in a still
small voice, and in terms we can understand. Sometimes, when you
are in the midst of all the proverbial "noises" of your situation, you
may have to dig deep to find that voice. I have found that if I take the
time to listen, I will hear it. Oh, yes, He *is* always with us! And, yes,
He *does* speak to us!

One Sunday afternoon, Jess, Charlie, Janet, and I went to the
home of longstanding church friends, Charlie and Eleanor Spreckles.
It was an afternoon of games, a potluck buffet, and fellowship. I really
was not up for the occasion, and did not want to go. However, I tried
hard to be agreeable for my sister who was so concerned for me, and
who asserted that I needed to be there. When I arrived, everyone was
chatting happily, and I just wanted to run away from there. I broke
down at one point and started to cry, running to the rest room to cry
in private. I knew some of the people there, but not everyone, and I
felt like a fish out of water. It had been a mere three weeks since I had
buried Bill, and I could not function socially. I hated that everyone
was so happy while my heart was so broken—not that I wished this
on them, but that I just was not yet ready to be with joyful banter. I

resented being with people who had no idea what my broken heart felt like, who couldn't even begin to fathom how shattered my world was, and who were so happy in the midst of my personal desolation. It was a very difficult situation for me to manage, but I did the best I could. These are really good people, and they did not deserve my resentment or irritation.

After the games and dinner, we sat around and sang some of the hymns of old. My sister played the piano, and everyone sang along. I could feel my spirit relaxing as God's presence filled that room. It was a very sweet, comforting, loving presence and it calmed and soothed me from within. When we were done singing, Charlie Spreckles explained my situation to everyone and asked them to pray for me. I bowed my head and closed my eyes as each person, one by one, prayed from their heart to God's on my behalf. I remember feeling so grateful for those prayers for I could not pray in the condition I was in, yet I knew I needed God's help more than I ever had. I was not angry with God. I dearly love Him. I still had my full faith placed in Him, but I was too shattered to be able to pray. I believe God knows that, and that is why we are commissioned to pray for each other.

During that prayer time, I could feel peace come to my soul. Somehow—and, I have no way to explain this—I knew I would be all right. I just knew it! The only way I can even begin to explain this is that I felt as if God had placed salve on the shards of my heart, and that my healing could, and would, now begin. I felt that no matter what lay ahead I would ultimately be okay. I just did not know how long this process would take, how I would actually get there, or how okay I would be. However, my faith was stronger than ever, and I clung to that faith for my very life, itself.

As we left Charlie and Eleanor's house, Charlie said something to me that I reminded myself of many times during the next year: "Don't live the rest of your life looking in the rear view mirror, Priscilla." I remember thinking at the time, *Hmmm…that is such a simple statement, yet so profound!* Little did I know how much I would need those simple words. Nor did I realize how often I would play them over in my mind whenever I looked back and wanted things to be as they had been before all this horror began. That was one of my toughest battles, and Charlie's words helped me greatly. When I had those, *I want things to be as they were and I want Bill back here with me* moments, I would remember Charlie's words and force myself to look to the future. I discovered that it is these conscious, deliberate decisions, however small, that help you recover. I knew that I did not want to be stuck here, that I could not live the rest of my life in this unbelievable pain. Therefore, I am forever grateful to Charlie for his wonderful words of wisdom because they helped me forge forward through some of the hardest moments of my grief journey.

More Gold Nuggets

*A*nother nugget of gold came from Nancy White, a dear friend of my sister's, and now mine. Nancy is one of those people I have admired from afar since I was a small child. She always seemed to know the right thing to do and say, and since I struggled with those two things, she was someone I wished I could have been like. The one thing I have come to understand about Nancy is how open her heart is, and how eagerly and honestly she is willing to share from her own experience to help others.

Nancy had lost her husband several years before, and she really seemed to understand where I was emotionally. She invited me to ask her any questions I had, and she made me feel completely comfortable asking them. She said she would answer all of them as best as she could. I am sure I asked many more questions than she had bargained for, but she was very patient and kind and answered each one completely and candidly. She stressed the uniqueness of the road I was on, and that I should understand that what had worked for her, may not work for me. But, she assured me that I *would* know what was right for me. She also repeatedly told me, "Priscilla, you will be fine! I can tell by the questions you're asking that you will be just fine!"

Nancy helped me more than she can ever imagine. During the next year of my journey, her words rang over and over in my brain. When I wanted to give up, feeling that this "grieving thing" was just way too hard and that I just was not going to be able to rise above it, I would hear Nancy's words: "Priscilla, you will be fine!" And, I would "see" her example: she was laughing and enjoying life again, she was socially engaged, and she was so well put together. Once again, I found myself fighting hard to be like her.

Charlie and Nancy—two wonderfully caring people whose simple statements got me through the worst of it. ...pure nuggets of gold!

Time to Leave

*D*uring my stay in New York, I saw a lot of family and friends, but I barely remember the visits. It is very strange to know you have been with someone, yet you do not remember that you actually *were* with that person nor can you recall what you discussed. "Auto pilot" is a great way your mind protects you from those unbearably painful experiences, yet you lose so much of life during those times. It makes me sad that I have lost so many great moments, yet I was in survival mode and I have no choice but to accept that.

Finally, it was time to leave. Saying, "good-bye" to my family was very difficult, so I promised them I would be back every year going forward. And, I meant to keep that promise! It is always easier to say, "Good-bye" when you know that at some pre-determined point in time, you will say, "Hello" again. I learned to do that when Vicki lived in New Jersey. I never left there without having decided on the next date I would be back. It made it easier for both of us to part. So, with lots of hugs, kisses, and tears, we said, "Good-bye." And, Janet and I backed out of Jess and Charlie's driveway. We were headed to Florida where we had planned to visit my cousin, Jimmie and his family, and some dear life-long friends.

On to Florida

*O*ne thing about me is that I am an adventurous person. I will pretty much drive anywhere. I shy away from Manhattan, however, because there really are no rules to the road there that either drivers or pedestrians follow. So, as we headed towards Florida, I diligently followed my GPS' instructions where, against all reason and logic, we found ourselves right in the heart of Manhattan. In fact, at one point, we were stopped at a red light and I looked up to try to figure out where we were. There we sat—right in front of the Empire State Building! "Oh My! *This* is a stress I truly do not need right now!" I bellowed loudly to Janet. "I have a rule about *not* driving in Manhattan!" I shouted. And, while *I* thought that navigating the Manhattan traffic was frustrating and stressful, *Janet* could not have been more pleased at seeing the Empire State Building! Since she had never been to this part of the country before, she was completely awed by the sights and amazingness of the place. It took us three (yes, three!) tries through the Midtown Tunnel before we finally figured out how to get onto the New Jersey Turnpike heading south.

As in all things I face, I can usually find humor in any given situation and this was no exception. Though we were stressed and frustrated, we found ourselves laughing at how awful that piece of the trip had been. Yet, we were so very happy that it was behind us, that we were finally on our way, and that Janet had been able to see the Empire State Building.

I do not remember very much about this trip except that the driving was much more difficult because I was so tired. The weather, on the other hand, was much nicer than it was on the trip up to New York. The sun was shining, and the temperature remained a wonderfully comfortable 80 degrees. Janet continued to be the perfect travel companion. We finally made it, with the GPS' help, right to the front door of my cousin's house.

What am I Doing Here?

immie saw us pull up, and came out of the house to greet us. It was so good to see him! We went into the house, met his two little Yorkies, and visited for a while. Janet and I were going to stay at a condominium of a relative of Jimmie's wife, Vinnie. After visiting for a while, Jimmie took us to our temporary home. Janet and I unpacked and settled in. Later that day, Jimmie picked us up and took us out to eat. I don't remember much about the visit, but I do remember that dinner! It was at a Chinese restaurant whose owner was from Chinatown in New York, and that was the best Chinese food I have ever eaten. I don't think I will ever forget that dinner! I remember asking the owner to open a restaurant in Katy, Texas but he was not amenable to the idea.

We had been invited to a get-together with some friends later that day. So, after dinner, Janet and I went to Mary Lou and Leo Caputo's house where Maria Linder, another friend, joined us. I have known Mary Lou and Maria since I was fifteen years old, and although it was very good to be with them, I really wasn't *there*. I remember that everyone was happily chatting and there was even a debate of some sort going on, but I didn't speak very much. In fact, I don't remember talking at all. My heart was so unbelievably raw and I felt very overwhelmed. The conversation kept becoming jumbled in my brain, and I wasn't able to sort through it. At some point, I started to sink emotionally. I simply could not function, I was not up for conversation, and I wanted to run away from there. I looked over and saw a recliner in the next room. I got up and walked over to it, sank into the recliner, and fell into a deep sleep. My girlfriend, Maria, woke me when she had to leave. Janet and I left, also, and returned to the condo. I had missed nearly the entire visit, and I greatly regret that, but it was the best I could do.

Jimmie and Vinnie made sightseeing plans with us for the next day, Saturday. Then on Sunday we were going to have a family dinner with them and their children. Janet and I were going to head back to Texas on Monday morning.

I am not sure what happened over night, but I woke up Saturday morning in a *really* bad place. I could not stop crying, and I told Janet that I had to go home. I just *had* to leave! I was restless and nervous, and as close to an anxiety attack as I will ever experience. I didn't know what to do. I didn't want to disappoint everyone, but I just couldn't stay, either. *What am I doing here?* I thought. *I need to be in my own home. I am done traveling—done!* I just wanted to be home where I could feel Bill's presence again, and to be with the things that were familiar and comfortable to me—the things that had been *ours*. I missed Bill so very much!

I talked to Janet about it, and she suggested that I call Jimmie and explain my situation to him. So, through my sobs, I made the call. Jimmie was very understanding and comforting. Vinnie got on the phone, as well. They reassured me that they understood, and that it was no problem if I left. They did ask that we have dinner with them before we headed out, and Vinnie graciously started cooking right away. A few hours later, we were at their home, and Janet and I were enjoying a scrumptious dinner with my wonderful cousin and his equally wonderful wife.

When dinner was over, Janet and I headed out. It had been a short, but really fantastic visit. I was, however, ready to go back home to Texas.

Home Again

We made it back to Katy in a day-and-a-half. I dropped Janet off at her house, and headed towards mine. What a wonderful sight to see my house again! No one was home, and I brought my suitcases in and laid down to rest. I was completely exhausted but so very grateful to be back in my own house again. A little while later, Vicki and the girls arrived. It was really good to see them again.

Vicki and her family had always planned to move out on their own, and this seemed like a good time to do that. I totally supported that decision. They had been with us for three years and had sacrificed their own home to help me care for Bill. All three girls had been sharing one bedroom and they were getting older and truly needed more space. They were "tripping" over each other in that room! I felt that it was best for the girls if they had something new and happy to anticipate. In their own home, each girl could have her own room and decorate it with all her pretty things, and have it arranged just as she wanted. They had dealt with so much sadness and loss since they had arrived and that really hurt my heart. So, I was glad they would have something fun to look forward to. About a week or so after I returned, they all moved out.

Tina really struggled with leaving, telling me, "Nanny, you'll be all alone." I reassured her that I would be fine, and that she would only be two minutes away and we would still see each other all the time. Very reluctantly, she complied. She did tell me every time she saw me, though, that she wanted to come back and live with me because I was all alone. I always reassured her that I was fine, but I never got the feeling that she really believed me. I knew she missed her Buddy—*really* missed him, and maybe that was part of her wanting to be with me.

Back to Work

*E*ven though my doctor had signed me out of work until July 8th, I felt I was ready to go back earlier. So, on June 23rd, I returned to work part-time. I was very anxious about going back to the office, wondering how I would react to being back in a very *normal* activity but being in such an *abnormal* place emotionally. I mean, my job and the people there were the same, but *I* was not. I was profoundly different. How was I going to manage that?

As I thought about returning to work, I knew I just could not handle a lot of people who, with the best of intentions, might flood me with questions I would not be able to answer without a lot of emotional pain and tears. I was very unsure of myself, but I knew I needed to get back to work if for nothing else, to help me get through the long, lonely days.

As with everything I do in life, I prayed about this. I asked God to help me put my life back together, and to give me the strength to face that life without Bill. I asked Him to help me to look forward so I would not keep looking back to what could never be anymore. I prayed for the courage to face my future and for the resolution to be actually able to walk into the hospital where I work. Then, I proceeded with the faith that God would help me. I arrived at the hospital, took a deep breath, and walked through the door. As I got off the elevator, I looked around, and no one was there. I was very grateful for that, sighing with relief. I was happy to be able to slip into my office quietly. Then, I saw her—one of the pathologists who had lost her mother around the same time I had lost Bill, walking down the hallway towards me. There is nothing or no one else who could have been more perfect for my first encounter! Once again, what appeared to be a coincidence was simply God's hand in taking care of me. He is SO amazing and awesome!

This pathologist and I hugged and cried, and there was an understanding of where we both were emotionally that no one else could have had. We had a short conversation about how neither of us was doing very well, and we walked down the hallway to the office area together. It was a very special moment for me, and I walked into my office with a more confident step.

Harsh Reality

I remember being in my office, sitting at my desk, and looking around. I felt very strange. I mean, everything looked familiar—the same, in fact, as I had left it ten weeks before. My job responsibilities were unchanged, the people I worked with were no different, and everything on my desk was exactly as it had always been. Even the paint on the walls was the same color it had been before I left. But, things weren't the same. *I* wasn't the same. My world wasn't the same. And, everything, though the same, felt very different. Then, I realized that there would be no calls from Bill that day, or the next day—or ever again. And, I closed my office door and cried.

An Abundance of Support

*A*lmost immediately, word got out that I was back and a steady stream of people came to see me. My fear of having to answer a lot of questions was quickly abated as each one came in and welcomed me back. Their smiles, hugs, I love you's, and offers of support gave me new insight into what a great group of people I work with. I was very grateful for each one who took the time out of his/ her busy day to stop by my office because I know that was not easy for them. They came because they are such deeply caring people. They had supported me through Bill's illness, and then they were there again afterwards to help me pick up the pieces of my life. They are more than just co-workers—they are my professional family.

About a day or two after I had returned to work, I was walking down the hallway. The locksmith, Anthony, saw me and we greeted each other. Then, he mentioned that he hadn't seen me in a while. I told him I had been out because "my husband passed away." He said, "You mean your mother, right?" So, I told him that my mother had passed away in January and my husband, in April. His entire expression changed to one of disbelief, and he shook his head and softly said, "I don't *even* know what to say, Priscilla!" I smiled understandingly, "You just said it, Anthony. Thank you!" I had gotten his message—heart to heart—no words were needed.

Land Mines

I discovered that when you lose someone you love, working your way through grief is a process—a journey. And, along that journey, you encounter situations that you could not have seen coming, but those encounters completely devastate you. A friend once referred to them as "land mines." I have to agree! You can prepare yourself for the "big" events, but there is absolutely no way you can prepare for those land mines. You may feel that you are having a fairly good day, you are managing your tears, maybe focusing better. You might even have managed to smile, and BAM! You find yourself in a sobbing, annihilated state fighting, once again, for your life!

I experienced this when I went to the store to purchase a birthday card for Joe. I had done that simple task thirty-seven times before, so I never gave it a second thought. I started to reach for a card, and my arm stopped in mid-air stretched out towards the row of cards. I could no longer buy cards for my children to "*Our* daughter" or to "*Our* son." BAM! It had been only two months since Bill had died, and I ran out of the store and into my car where I sobbed uncontrollably. I had hit a land mine.

Land mines, I discovered, are long lasting and mega-strong at first. They come often and hard and sometimes on top of each other. And each time you hit one it takes what feels like forever to recover from it. At first, they are all around you—memories at each turn and everywhere you look. You cry a lot in the beginning because *everything* is a reminder of what you no longer have. You are barely over the first land mine when you hit the next one. It is so unbelievably hard to manage these at first. But, as you continue your journey to recovery, those moments come farther apart and are not as devastating, nor do they take as long to recover from. I remember getting through my first day without one and thinking, "Hmmm... I didn't hit one today!" It was both a good and a sad feeling. Good because that meant my heart was truly healing. But it was also sad, because it made me realize that I was actually creating a life without Bill. And, even though it made me sad, I knew that that was what Bill wanted me to do. He wanted me to be "good" again. He had told me, in fact, that he wanted me to rebuild my life. He said I was free to find someone else, someone who would love me and be good to me, and who would make me happy. That was his last gift to me. Bill did not want me to feel guilty about rebuilding my life. What an amazing gift from a remarkable man!

I learned that it is okay to cry when you need to. As I hit each land mine, I cried my way through it, dried my tears, and kept going. That worked for me. My family and friends knew I would have those "moments," and they would give me a hug, or not, but didn't make a big deal about it. When I was through crying, I would rejoin the conversation or whatever we had been doing before the "hit." That is exactly how I needed it. I told everyone, "I'll be fine. Just give me time to work through it. It's just how it is right now." And, they complied, which made it much easier for me, though I know it was difficult for them to see me like that. I was always the one who brought laughter, not tears, to our get-togethers. This was so out of character for me that I could see the pain in their eyes as they watched me suffer through those moments.

It took about a year, but the land mines slowly became more like potholes. You hit one, you're shaken up for a few seconds, or you may cry for a minute or two. Then it is over. You dust yourself off and you keep going. They are much farther apart and more easily manageable. I am so very grateful for that!

Going from "Ours" to "Mine"

I decided that if I was to be able to rebuild my life emotionally, I had to make some changes to my "world," as well. I decided to do three things to my house: paint the entire interior, replace the carpeting throughout, and get a new bedroom set. It was just too hard to be in the house exactly as it was when Bill was there. There were too many memories of him being so sick and suffering so much. I knew I would have to make these changes to make the house "mine" if I was going to be able to be at peace in it. This sounded like a good idea on paper. When I tried to implement the plan, though, I realized I was not ready for the upheaval it would cause. I had set the plan in motion, however, so I had no choice but to forge ahead.

I had to begin by taking everything off the walls and removing everything off the floors because the house was being painted *and* carpeted. This was a huge undertaking at a time when I had no strength, I was completely overwhelmed by grief, and I was exhausted all the time. My wonderful daughter-in-law, Lisa, and her best friend, Wendy, offered to assist me and they were amazingly helpful. They packed everything up and carried all the boxes to the garage. I actually did very little because they took care of it all. I am forever grateful to them. I absolutely could not have done that without them!

With the house ready, the painters showed up. Each night when I returned home from work, I noticed that there was less maneuvering space in the house as the painters moved the furniture around to get to the walls. Blinds were on the floor, paint cans were everywhere, and my house was a total disaster. After the third night, I had a meltdown. "Have I not been through enough?" I screamed to no one. Everything in my life was in shambles and I did not need my house to be a mess, too. I could not handle it! I was sinking lower instead of starting my ascent from the "pit" I was in. I wanted a "do over" going back to when Bill was alive and not having him die—back to when he was young and healthy and we were so happy, but that wasn't possible. I was so frustrated! I called Vicki and between my sobs, I told her I could not do this.

Vicki has a very calming, reassuring approach to people, and she told me to pack a bag and stay with her for a few days. I agreed, but getting to my clothes was a huge challenge for me. I had to climb over furniture, blinds, paint cans, tools, and ladders to get to the bedroom. Once my bags were packed, I had to trek back over the hurdles, *again*, to get to the front of the house. Only this time I had my bags to carry, as well. It was a very low point for me, and I was not handling it very well.

I drove to Vicki's house where I stayed until the painting was done. I was really fighting depression at this point, and losing the battle. My grief counselor kept in close touch with me, and I really needed that. I am not a person who suffers from chronic depression as Bill did, so this was a new "place" for me. And, it was a frightening place—because no matter what I did, I just could not pull myself up out of it. I kept fighting, though, because I wanted to be whole again. …needed to be!

Project "Mine" Continues

*T*he carpeting project was a lot easier on me than the painting venture. The carpet installers were in and out of the house in one day. When they were done, the effect in the house was absolutely wonderful. I was very pleased with the way the carpet matched the wall color, and my home seemed to come alive with these two "touches." I had made a good decision, and I was very pleased!

Having to face getting everything unpacked, hung back on the walls, and placed back in the house again was overwhelming. But Joe, Lisa, and Wendy were my "life savers." They devoted many hours to help me settle back in and to make my house "home" again. And, because of their unselfish efforts, I had my home back. It was different, yet the same and I could live there in peace. I had to smile.

A New Bedroom Set

*O*ne thing I needed to do to help me build my new life was to replace my bedroom set. I just couldn't sleep in my bed—not because Bill had died there, but because he had lived there. It was just too difficult to look at that furniture and remember how we shopped for it together right before we were married. It had been with us from the beginning and was with us through our entire marriage. I simply could not keep it. It was too painful to look at. Besides, having it in my home where I saw it every day caused me to keep looking backward instead of forward, inhibiting my ability to allow my heart to heal. Therefore, one afternoon, Vicki took me shopping and I found a bedroom set I fell in love with.

The time came for the delivery of the new set. Well, I should have known when the store gave me a delivery window of 7:00 a.m. to 10:00 p.m. that things were probably not going to go smoothly. Liz, my sister, offered to stay with me and I welcomed her visit enthusiastically. At least, if I had to be in the house the entire day, I would have some company. Finally, at around 6:00 p.m., the truck arrived. I was so excited! I felt like a child waiting for Christmas! However, my excitement quickly vanished when the person putting the bed together asked me where the slats were. "HUH," I asked! "Don't *you* have those?" He replied that I had to purchase them, and if I had not paid for them, then they would not be included with the bed. I absolutely could not believe it! No one had told me that! I was furious! That was one more thing to deal with at a time when I couldn't deal with *anything*! The road I was on, I thought to myself, was exponentially harder than I could ever have imagined!

I called Joe and asked him to help me. I just did not know what to do, and I could not handle one more stress. Joe came to the rescue, and after a couple of hours, another truck showed up with the slats. My world was good once more! But, it didn't take long for things to go south again, when the new person putting the bed together came to me and asked me if I had the hardware. I absolutely could not believe it! Were they kidding me? I called customer support and the person on the phone told me that they would mail the hardware to me and I should have it in a week to ten days. Once I had the hardware, I was told, I could then reschedule a time for the workers to return and complete putting my bed together. I was at my breaking point! This was much more than I could manage. Once again, I called Joe, and he came "unglued!" He told me not to worry, that I *would* sleep in my bed "tonight!" They were not going to disrespect his mother like that! I do not know what Joe said but I suspect he morphed into "Guido." Right before 10:00 p.m., the manager of the warehouse knocked on my door, hardware in hand. After a short while, my bed was together, and Liz helped me put the bedding on it. I was so happy. My bedroom looked beautiful, and I just knew I would sleep much more peacefully with the changes I had made.

More Stress

wo to three weeks after I got my bedroom set, I had Vicki and the girls over for dinner. However, because my only two brain cells that were working at the time were not firing at the same time, I'd had all my furniture, including the kitchen and dining room chairs, steam cleaned that day. Great!

So, I told the girls we would have a picnic. I put some tablecloths on my bed and we were going to get our food and eat on the bed. The plan, I thought, was a good one and everyone was enjoying the fun we were having. We started to get on the bed, and all of a sudden—BAM! The bed collapsed on one side and the frame broke into what looked like long, thin matchsticks. I absolutely, positively, without a shadow of a doubt, could not believe it! I was livid! I called customer service once again, but this time *I* blasted the person who answered the phone. *I* became "Guido!"

It took about five days, but they did send their repairperson out. My dear friend, Rosemary, offered to be at the house to be sure they took care of the problem properly. I just was not up for handling it, and I was very grateful for her offer. It was determined that the delivery people used neither the correct slats nor the right hardware, so that is why the bed broke. The repair people fixed the bed, and Rosemary insisted that they replace the frame on both sides of the bed, as well. They easily complied. I am sure they did not want to deal with "Ms. Guido" again.

The good news is that the bed has been just fine with the correct slats and hardware, and my bedroom looks really beautiful. I am very much at peace there.

Lessons Learned

*L*ooking forward, you do not always see the potential flaws in your decisions, especially when you are grieving. You think you are making logical, rational decisions, but you really are incapable of that. Looking back, however, always brings 20/20 vision. If I had to do this again, I would not take on any huge projects while in the throes of deep grief. It was more, much more, than I could handle. Had everything gone smoothly, it would have been a challenge! But, when you factor in the additional misery caused by the snags, it caused me to become more anxious and stressed than I needed to be, and made me continue my emotional decline. I made a mental "note to self": *no big projects while deeply grieving. Wait until you are in a better emotional place.*

A Deep, Dark Place

I was slowly rebuilding my life, one component at a time. I could not handle more than that. I found it interesting that life just guides you into knowing what you need to do. I thought about that a lot. I reflected on how innately the knowledge is within us. What an amazing realization that was! God gives us the tools we need to meet and recover from life's traumas even before we know we will need those tools. WOW! I mean, first I completed my trip to New York, and then I was able to go back to work. Afterwards, I completed my remodeling project, and then I was able to return to church. I was glad I was able to add things back into my life—even just one at a time. I felt that was very positive. And, people were commenting about how remarkably well I was doing. My grief counselor stated it, the people who supported me in the Grief Recovery Method® group mentioned it, and the doctors I worked with commented on it. My friends even said it. I remember thinking that if this was doing well, what does it feel like to be doing poorly? My brain could not even go there!

Since it is very tempting to isolate during this phase, I really had to fight not to do that. You just do not want to be with others because you barely have enough energy to function, and socializing just takes too much out of you. Life is a huge effort at this point, and I found myself passing on many invitations. Even when I accepted, I always qualified my "yes" with "however, I may not be able to be there."

Friends and family were very understanding and that really helped me until I was able to engage socially again.

Everyone thought I was doing great. But, I knew I wasn't—not even close! Yes, I *was* making progress, but coming home from work to an empty, dark, silent house was *so* unbelievably hard! I loved going to work, but at the end of the day, I dreaded coming home. I had gone from having seven of us in the house, to just me. The emptiness and the silence were oppressive and deafening. I absolutely hated opening the front door every evening because I was greeted with a very loud *nothing.* My house just screamed "death" to me and was a constant reminder that Bill was gone and that all that was left was a huge, hollow space where he had once been. I absolutely could not handle that. My children hovered closely and friends and family stayed near, but at the end of the day—when everyone left and I locked my front door—it was just me in the thick, dark, deafening silence of my home.

No matter how much I tried, I could not stop the emotional slide on which I found myself. I was fighting really hard to find something—anything—that would stop the decline, but I couldn't find it. I was frightened, alone, and unequivocally depressed.

One Saturday afternoon in July, I was sitting on my couch and I could feel myself emotionally spiraling downward. I could not stop it! I realized that I was headed to a place where, if I actually reached it, would cause me to do something really dreadful. I did not want to live any more—not like this! This was a cold, dark, harsh, lonely, painful place and I could not stay here. I just *couldn't*! But, I could not help myself up out of it, either. The only way out, I thought, was that I would have to end my life. I had reached such a low place that I did not even think about the affect this action would have on my children and grandchildren. I never even thought about them. And, even though I had cautioned Bill about this very thing, I wasn't able to recall my own words. On some deep level, though, I knew this should not, could not, happen. It went against everything I had been taught and what I believed. How would I face God knowing I had taken the life He had so graciously given me? That thought brought instant, all-consuming terror to my heart. I knew I desperately needed help. And, I needed it quickly! I immediately reached for the phone and called Donna, my grief counselor. She could hear the angst in my voice and I cried as I told her where I was emotionally, and where I was headed. I was afraid. I was lonely. I was suffering. I was slipping into deeper darkness. And, I could not stop the downward decline.

My Own Little Buddy

*D*onna let me get it all out, and when I had stopped talking, she said she had a suggestion for me that she felt would help me. "Priscilla," she said, "you're alone in the house. You need a pet." "A pet?" I asked, surprised that she did not offer me a more profound solution. "Yes," she said, "and you should consider naming it Buddy. Buddy isn't a pet name *you* had for Bill, but hearing it may be comforting to you." I thought about Donna's suggestion and it made a lot of sense. I have always preferred dogs to cats, so I thought I would get a dog—a Yorkie, because I had fallen in love with Jimmie's two Yorkies when I was in Florida.

I called Janet, and she put me in contact with an excellent breeder. I called the breeder, and after she interviewed me on the phone, she told me she had the perfect dog for me—a four-month-old female Yorkie that she had planned to show. She said this dog's temperament is just perfect for me. The dog is sweet and calm and would be a good companion. So, I arranged for us to meet the breeder in Dallas to get my new puppy. Four of us took that trip: Vicki, Janet, Janet's daughter, Janie, and me.

We arrived at the "drop off" point, and when the breeder got out of her car with the dog, I reached out and took the dog into my arms. I was instantly in love! How could a little four-pound creature fill my heart so much? She was *so* unbelievably cute, and so incredibly sweet! She was calm and quiet and not "yippy" at all. The breeder had been right. She was perfect for me! Vicki drove home, and I held my little one in my arms the entire five-hour trip. Petting her was so comforting, and I started to feel better almost immediately.

I thought about what to name her. And, I decided on "Buddy Rose." I thought the "Buddy" part would be good for Tina. She could come over and have a new buddy to play with. That might help her adjust a little easier to not having her Buddy here. I added "Rose" so everyone would know that she is a girl. It worked for me!

Buddy Rose was a Godsend. As small as she was, she filled my home and my heart with love. She saved my life! Someone asked me why she was so special, because I'd had other dogs before. I told that person that I *wanted* the other dogs, but this one, I *needed*. I had looked suicide in the face—eyeball to eyeball—and I had survived. My little Buddy Rose had made all the difference!

Buddy Rose and I have settled into a wonderful routine together. When I get home from work in the evenings, she runs around the living room and is so excited to see me. Bill was never *that* happy to see me! Then, we go back to my bathroom where I check the puppy pad to see if she was a good girl. If she was, she gets a treat, which she always gets. She then rolls over and wants me to rub her tummy. It is a wonderful time for both of us and she is so cute, she makes me laugh. After dinner, she curls up on my lap while I read, write, or watch a little TV. I love to pet her. It is so healing.

I have learned the great value of the human touch through this, and I now hug people much more easily. Do you know the best thing about a hug? You cannot give one without getting one back! It's the best!

I'm SO Angry!!

A couple of weeks after I got Buddy Rose, I found myself consumed with anger. I remember waking up on a Saturday morning and I just did not know what to do with how I was feeling. It was all consuming and incredibly strong! I started to cry—sob, in fact—and could not stop. I walked around my house and saw all of Bill's touches: a picture he had hung, gifts he had given me, the map of Long Island that he loved so much. And I was, once again, devastated. I remember walking into my kitchen and screaming at the very top of my lungs, "YOU WERE SUPPOSED TO GROW OLD WITH ME! I CAN'T DO THIS WITHOUT YOU! THIS IS JUST TOO HARD TO DO ALONE!"

I felt that I had lost all the progress I had made. I thought I was back to square one only now it included overwhelming anger. My heart was so broken and so raw and I missed Bill so very much. Nothing made sense any more, and I desperately needed life to be right again. As I continued to sob, a thought came to me: *Do you want him back?* I remember screaming to no one in particular, "NO, I DON'T WANT HIM BACK! WHY WOULD I WANT HIM TO LEAVE HEAVEN? I JUST DIDN'T WANT HIM TO GO IN THE FIRST PLACE!"

After some time, I settled down but the anger remained. I battled it the entire weekend. I went to church that Sunday and one of the women greeted me and asked me if I was doing all right. I remember shaking my head "no." I started crying, and I ran out of the building to my car. When I got to work on Monday, I called my friend, Pam Taylor, the hospital's senior chaplain. She could hear the emotion in my voice, and told me to come right to her office. I told her how angry I was, but honestly, she could easily see it. I also said that I did not know what to do about it. She encouraged me to get it all out, to say whatever I needed to say, to let it go. She asked me if I was angry with Bill. "No," I said through my sobs. "Bill had no control over what happened to him. I'm not angry with him!" Then, I added, "I'm not angry with God, either." She smiled and told me that was her next question. "God is sovereign," I told her. "I am not angry with Him. I am just angry!"

"Then, where do you think your anger is coming from, Priscilla?" she asked. "I'm angry," I told her, "because Bill and I were supposed to grow old together. We were supposed to see our granddaughters grow up, graduate from high school and college, get married, have babies, etc. We built our house together, our last house! We were *both* supposed to be living in it. I wasn't supposed to be living there alone!"

Talking things out with Pam made me realize that I was angry that I had lost my future with Bill. Up to that point, I had been mourning the loss of the memories Bill and I had made in the past. But that weekend, I faced the loss of the memories we would never get to make in the future. That was an enlightening moment, and having worked through the anger, and understanding the reasons for it, helped me greatly. I left Pam's office feeling calmer, knowing I had completed another step in my grief recovery.

Ring or No Ring

Four months after Bill's death I was still wearing my ring, the ring Bill had given me for our Twenty-Fifth wedding anniversary. I wore that ring as if it was my wedding ring because a thief who had come into our New York home one night years before had stolen the original ring. I had asked Nancy what to do about my ring when I was in New York, and she had assured me that I would know when the time was right for me to take it off, or if I wanted to leave it on.

I found that as time went on, it became more and more painful to put that ring on. Each morning, when I reached for the ring, my heart would break all over again. It was a daily reminder of everything I had lost, and I knew my heart could not fully recover if I kept reopening that wound. One day in early September, I put the ring on—then reluctantly took it off again. It was much less painful not to continue that ritual. I held the ring close to my heart, whispered to Bill, "it's time…," and cried as I tucked the ring away. I had reached another milestone in my recovery from grief.

A Slow Ascent

My recovery was a slow, steady ascent from the darkness. Some days I took one step forward and two back, but other days I was able to move forward—even just one tiny step. I thought about how I was in the "valley of the *shadow* of death." Bill had walked that valley of death, but I was definitely in its shadow. I discovered that the verse in Psalm 23:4 (KJV) "Yea, though I walk through the valley of the shadow of death, I will fear no evil: for thou art with me; thy rod and thy staff they comfort me" was really for the survivor.

That valley is a dark, cold, lonely place filled with overwhelming fear. Things that I normally would not think about weighed heavily on my mind and I worried constantly. How am I going to be able to pay my mortgage? How will I know the right decision to make without being able to bounce my ideas off Bill? What if I got sick? Who will be with me to care for me and to comfort me? What if I died? I would be all alone and the kids wouldn't know I was gone until the next day. Fear upon fear gripped my soul. It was the hardest place I had ever been in my entire life! And, even though I was functioning again, I could not completely seem to make my way out of that horrific place. I fought really hard to come out, and because of that, I *was* making progress, but the progress wasn't quick enough for me. I really struggled with the fear. Everything I did was overshadowed by it, and I suffered. I asked God to help me through this. I pictured myself like a child, being held by the Lord, close to his chest, and comforted by Him. That visual and the promise in Psalm 23:4 got me through this place. I *knew* the Lord was with me. I could feel His presence, His peace. I felt God's love more intensely than I ever had and I was greatly comforted by that. That verse became especially real to me. And, for the first time in my life, I embraced it and truly understood it. Yes, I had received new insight about darkness and fear, but I had also been given the special gift of knowing God's wonderful love and comfort.

I repeated that verse over and over in my head and sometimes I said it aloud. I listened to my Gospel music, which uplifted my spirit. I used the tools I had learned in the Grief Recovery Method® program, and I kept in touch with my grief counselor. I was fighting hard for my life—HARD!

Progress

$\mathcal{A}$s the days and months went by, I found myself being able to engage more in life. I started to feel alive, a little at a time. I laughed again and was able to find humor in everyday situations once more. That was really important to me. I have always enjoyed humor and laughter. It is not only healing to me, but it is large part of who I am. So, losing that part of me made the journey much more difficult. The first time I laughed, I also cried. It felt so good to have *me* back. That was a huge moment for me because I thought I would never be able to laugh ever again.

I had created a new routine at home, and being alone didn't feel so unnatural anymore. I was "finding my feet" and it felt good. I was hopeful that eventually, life would be good again. And, even though I wasn't there yet, I could see the progress I was making and I was encouraged by that. Each step of advancement, no matter how miniscule, gave me the courage to keep going.

I also became acutely aware of the pain others were suffering as they walked their own path of challenges. And I thought about the fact that I completely understood how unbelievably hard that journey can be. So, I decided to reach out to those folks. I offered my hand of camaraderie and committed to support them when their road became particularly difficult. And, an amazing thing happened! I realized that as I reached out to help those individuals, my own heart was healing. What a revelation that was! I had always tried to be there to support people who were struggling. But I had discovered that when we are willing to give of ourselves while in the midst of our own great need, we receive, as well. Our natural tendency is to withdraw, feeling that we are unable to give because this is our time for others to care for us. However, if we are able to rise above that and offer our hand of friendship—especially when things are the most arduous for us, we are blessed with God's amazing grace and care in ways we could never have imagined.

There were still difficult days to deal with—birthdays, anniversaries, holidays. The "firsts" are the most difficult. I got through each one of those by accepting my sadness and crying whenever I needed to. Everyone was really understanding and supportive, knowing that the sun would come up for me again "tomorrow."

Christmas was especially hard because that was Bill's favorite holiday. He had always put up all the decorations inside and outside the house, and took such delight in doing so. He had some sleigh bells that he said came from his grandfather's farm, and he loved putting them on the front door so they jingled whenever anyone opened that door. When everything had been put up, hung up, or arranged in its rightful place, Bill would ring those sleigh bells to gather us all together for the "lighting ceremony." He couldn't help but smile broadly as we "oohed and aahed" when everything lit up. I cherish those memories dearly.

The first year without him, though, I just could not face Christmas and I really struggled with how I was going to get through the holiday. I wanted to leave the planet on December 24th and return again on the 26th. I told everyone that I wasn't even going to put a tree up because Bill had always done that. His last Christmas here, he was too sick to decorate or to put the tree together. He was even too weak to get the boxes out from the closet, and that made him feel so sad. The year before, the girls had worked with him as they all hung our beautiful decorations on the tree, making it look so magical. The gold and crystal ornaments and the golden ribbon that Bill so carefully wound around the tree it gave an elegant, yet festive appearance. They were all so happy and excited and Bill could not help but laugh at the fun they had all been having together. His last Christmas, I tried to help him manage the pain of not being able to participate actively in decorating the tree. I suggested that he teach the girls how to decorate it. I told him he could give them directions verbally and that, by doing so, he would leave them with a great legacy. I told him that for the rest of their lives, every time they put up their own Christmas tree, they would think of him because he had taught them how to do it. He was so sad that he was not able to participate actively, but he took my advice and guided those six little hands to perfection from his wheelchair. The tree was as beautiful as if he had done the work himself. The girls were proud of that tree. Bill was proud of the girls. And, I was proud of Bill for handling that painful moment so well. I still smile when I think of that tree! The first Christmas without him, however, would have to be without a tree. There would be no decorations, either. I just could not manage it physically or emotionally. I was feeling really sad again, only I knew it was temporary and that I would feel better after the holidays were behind me.

One of my employees, Cyndi, whose heart hurt for me, came into my office one day with a package. She was very apologetic as she told me that she had been watching me suffer about the Christmas tree. Therefore, she had gone and bought a small table tree for me that she wanted me to have. She said it was okay if I could not put it up, but she wanted me to have it anyway. She had even bought the decorations for it. I was so moved by that enormous gesture of kindness. I cried and hugged her, and thanked her for the tree, which I promised I would put on my coffee table. I got the tree halfway decorated, then had to stop. I just could not manage my pain. But, because of Cyndi's loving act of kindness, I did have a tree in my house that Christmas!

My journey included many of those kinds of special moments at work. One morning I was working at my desk when another employee, Ena, came in and told me, "You need a hug." Little did she know how much I needed it! Her heart had reached out to mine, and I stood up and accepted her hug. What love I received from my staff! They are amazing women—filled with compassion, love, and generosity. And, I have been the recipient of those wonderful acts of kindness over and over again, as I've walked this road. They all—every single one—played a huge role in my recovery. One of my employees, Dulce, brought me little surprises every so often: a cup of coffee, some fruit, and a special treat she thought I would enjoy. Another one of my employees, Karen, still, to this very day, gives me a hug every single morning. I look forward to those hugs, because they speak louder than any words could. They are right from her heart to mine! Peggy, another member of my team, hovered closely through this entire ordeal. Not a Monday went by without her coming into my office and asking me how my weekend was. During the worst of Bill's decline and after I returned to work, Peggy's care gave me perspective and strength. I am forever grateful to this wonderful group of women. I am very blessed, indeed!

Life is Good!

*O*ne morning in March, 2011 I woke up feeling really good. The darkness was gone, I had joy in my heart, and my step was lighter. I knew I had come out of the valley. It was an amazing moment, and I thanked God for His wonderful love and care through it all. That moment occurred eleven months after Bill died. My journey, though much more profoundly difficult than I could ever have imagined, had been relatively short. I will always be grateful for that!

Nahum 1:7 (NASB) tells us "The Lord is good, a stronghold in the day of trouble, and He knows those who take refuge in Him." I can attest to that! Not one second through my journey did I fail to feel His presence and His love. And the strength that carried me through could only have come from Him. I can never thank Him enough.

Around the time I came out of the valley, I began to write this book. As I shared my story and Bill's vision/experience with people— old friends and new, they encouraged me to "get it down on paper." So many people told me that others would need to hear this to help them on their journey, and that I really needed to write a book about it. I knew it would be hard to go back to those horrifically painful places now that I was back "with the living," but I did it because I truly want to help others. I was greatly rewarded, however, by having my own healing progress, as well. I am "good to go" now! And,

I am determined to help other people who have also experienced profound loss. In February, 2011, I became a Certified Grief Recovery Specialist® through the Grief Recovery Institute® of Sherman Oaks, California. I am looking forward to making a positive difference in the grief journey of others.

One More Hurdle

As well as I was doing, though, there was one more hurdle I had to manage: the first anniversary of Bill's death, April 28, 2011. The sadness set in about a week before that date, and I dreaded facing the day. I had been doing so well and the sadness was really difficult for me to deal with again. But, I had learned that there *are* going to be days like that and I *would* come out of it again.

I took the day off from work, and Vicki, Tina, and I planned the day. We would start by getting flowers, and then going to the cemetery. Afterwards, we would drive to Brenham, Texas and tour the Blue Bell factory in honor of Bill. We were all sad, and I wondered how long it would take for the sadness to lift since this was a major anniversary for us. Now that I'd been out of the darkness, I had no idea how days like this affect you or how long it would take to be "good" again.

We got up early that morning and stopped at the store where I bought a beautiful bouquet of flowers. Tina asked me if she could "put the flowers on my Buddy's grave," and I told her I thought that was a wonderful idea as I handed them to her to hold. The drive to the cemetery was a quiet one. We were all very subdued.

When we got to Bill's gravesite, we discovered that they were watering the grass—with those huge commercial sprinklers—five of them! Vicki thought we were not going to be able to visit his grave, but I said, "No, we *can* visit it! We can walk between the sprays of water. We'll be fine!" The one thing I did not factor into my decision was that those five long-range sprinklers were all rotating in different directions as they watered a huge area of grass.

We made our way to Bill's grave and all of a sudden, one of those sprinklers hit me on my back and completely soaked me. Then, one hit Vicki, and within seconds, Tina was completely drenched! We were trying to run between the sprays of water so we could spend some time at Bill's grave, but it just was not possible! We looked like three drowned rats that were crazily running around in all directions! Poor Tina had to literally throw the flowers at the grave as we ran for our lives—three laughing, squealing, soaked-to-the-bone "little girls!" Even the guy mowing the lawn on the other side of the street was laughing at us!

We got back to the car, and collapsed in hysterical laughter. Vicki had decided that Bill had planned that. Bill not only had an amazing sense of wit and humor, but he loved practical jokes, as well. I decided that it was Bill's way of telling us that the time for mourning was over, and we needed to laugh and enjoy life again. I have no doubt about that! And, yes, I had gotten his message!

The sadness lifted immediately for all of us, and because of the hot Texas weather, we dried off fairly quickly. We drove to the Blue Bell factory happily chatting and laughing along the way. We all enjoyed the tour, especially Tina who was fascinated watching the ice cream containers that she had seen in the grocery store being filled with her Buddy's favorite vice. The day turned out to be absolutely wonderful! At the end of the tour there was a free dish of our favorite flavor of ice cream. As we sat in the little Blue Bell shop and enjoyed our delectable treat, I could not help but smile as I thought about how much Bill would have really enjoyed that day.

My Promise

efore he died, I had promised Bill that we would never forget him no matter where life would take us. I had told him that every year on his birthday we would all get together and have a "Blue Bell Bash" in his honor. He was moved by that, and he smiled as he thanked me. I could tell it meant a lot to him.

So, on May 10, 2011, I invited the kids and their families over along with some friends. We barbecued hamburgers and had a nice dinner together. Following dinner, I had several half gallons of different flavors of Blue Bell ice cream. We all ate ice cream sundaes and talked about one favorite memory of Bill we each had. It was a wonderful evening in honor of Bill, and it gave me such joy. When the evening was over and everyone started to leave, Tina went outside, looked up to the sky, and yelled, "HAPPY BIRTHDAY, BUDDY" as loudly as she could. I'd like to think he heard her, and that he smiled sweetly at the message from his Little Buddy.

Full Circle

*I*n August, 2011, fifteen months after my trip to New York following Bill's funeral, I went back to New York again. I had promised my family that I would visit every year, and I will keep that promise. This time, though, I was very happy to go back. I wanted everyone to see how well I was doing, and I wanted to thank everyone who had played a role in my recovery.

It was a very special trip for me. Thanks to the coordination efforts of my sister, Jess, I did have an opportunity to see everyone who had helped me. I had a chance to thank the people who had prayed for me that Sunday at Charlie and Eleanor's house. I saw Charlie Spreckles and thanked him for his words of wisdom, and I told him how I clung to those words during the worst of my journey. He, in turn, thanked me for sharing that with him for it helped him to know that his work as a grief counselor really does make a difference. I shared with Nancy how much she had helped me. It wasn't only her words, but her living example that gave me the courage to keep fighting to come back. We both hugged and cried. She had no idea that her words would play such a huge role in my recovery. She was very moved by that.

I had many chances to thank my family and friends, and to show them how fully "good" I am. Whenever anyone asked me how I was, my answer was the same, "I'm GOOD—*really* GOOD!" We had many great moments of laughter as I shared some of my stories with them with my usual humorous slant. I have this silly, sometimes sarcastic sense of humor that I just cannot help expressing when I relate an experience I have had. I am back! I know it, and now everyone else knows it!

The Last Hurdle – The Closet

*A*s great as I was doing, there was still the last hurdle I had not conquered. From the moment Bill died through my entire grief journey of eleven months and the nine months following, there was one thing I could not face: cleaning the clothes out of Bill's closet. I remember looking into his closet shortly after the funeral and being unable to enter it. I preferred, instead, to stand at the doorway, afraid to walk forward. How do you even begin to think about getting rid of the clothes that still smelled of his cologne, that had been warmed by his body heat, and the shoes that were molded to the shape of his feet? I could recall each particular occasion that he wore every single item. And, looking at the clothes he wore the last year or so of his life, his *sick clothes* as I had come to refer to them, hurt my heart more deeply than I can ever express. He had suffered so much and it pained my heart profoundly to recall that phase of his life. The memories of him wearing those clothes were as vivid in my mind at that moment as if they had just been worn. Each shirt, tie, pair of slacks, and shoe became the most precious of treasures to me. They had to stay! There was no way I was going to give those away!

I had decided from the beginning of this long ordeal that my first goal was going to have to be to take care of "Priscilla." Until I was back to being myself again, until my heart was healed and I was *living* again, and until I was emotionally strong enough, this chore would have to wait. Being fortunate enough to have had separate closets, I simply closed that door and did not open it for the entire twenty-month period. I knew that at some point, I would have to tackle that task. And I had to trust that I would know when that time was right. Until then, however, the closet stayed as it was and the door remained closed.

Now that I had come out of that dark place and returned to the living, I started to think about *the closet*. Many times during that time period, I would walk by that door and place my hand on the knob but I could not turn it. I just could not enter what had become a very sacred yet dreadfully foreboding place. I was totally unable to look at the contents of that room. Months passed and I had made no progress on this even though I thought about it all the time. I kept feeling that I would face it at some point but I did not know how I was going to accomplish what was the last hurdle of my grief work. Friends and family offered to clean the closet for me but I felt that I had to be the one who had to complete that task. I had so diligently and so meticulously taken the best care of Bill that I could, and I felt that this would be the last thing I could do for him. Besides, Bill was a very private person and had he been alive, he would not have wanted anyone going through his personal belongings but me. So, I made the deliberate choice to respect him and his memory by being the one to handle this project, as hard as I felt it was going to be.

As the holidays of 2011 approached, this impending project began to weigh heavily on me. I had really been enjoying the excitement and joy of the holidays and visiting with family and friends without the pain of the previous year's grief. But in the back of my mind, I knew this was the last piece of letting go that I had to face if I was to be one hundred percent free to move on to the new adventures life would have to offer me. I wanted to be able to think about Bill as the huge part of my life that he was, without having any remaining encumbrances to the pain.

I mentioned this to Joe one day and he could see the sadness in my eyes as I told him I had set a goal to accomplish this task before the second anniversary of his Dad's death in April, 2012. I felt that if I did not pack up those clothes and give them away, then I was still holding on to the past and would not be fully able to embrace my future. Because of the wonderfully caring person Joe is, he offered to take this chore on for me. I stood my ground, however, telling him that *I* had to do it. This was a personal accomplishment that I had to achieve—me alone!

The first weekend following the New Year was one that was completely available to me. I had no meetings, appointments, social engagements, or deadlines. Nothing was on my agenda that I had to do nor did I have to be at any other place. So, on Saturday, January 7, 2012, I decided to start by cleaning out *my* closet. Since I had lost my mother in January 2010 and then Bill just three months later, I had begun the practice of putting things into my closet where they were safe but out of my sight. Things I could not handle or emotionally manage at the time were sent there. That worked well initially but nearly two years later, I couldn't even walk into my closet without stepping over a myriad of items and several large stacks of papers. So, after my morning coffee that Saturday, I got dressed and headed back to the dreaded mess I had created. One item at a time, I began the purge. Before too long, I had everything cleaned off that floor and could actually walk into the closet and get to the clothes on the hangers without tripping over anything. I was very pleased! I had done a good job, I thought to myself! Feeling tired after working nearly the entire day in that closet, I decided to tackle the four bags in the back of the closet the next day, Sunday.

On January 8, 2012, I went to church then out to dinner with Joe and Lisa and some friends. We all enjoyed a great visit and I returned home smiling because I was feeling so good, and ready to deal with those four bags—the bags from the funeral home. The first bag contained items from my mother's funeral. I felt my heart break again as I looked at the program, her death certificate, and other pertinent papers that had been placed in that bag. I had not really taken the time to mourn the loss of my mother because of all I was dealing with since Bill was declining so quickly at the time she had died. One by one, I took each bag out of my closet and went through its contents. Going through the bags from Bill's funeral was especially hard, and I cried as I read the kids' eulogies, the funeral program that contained Bill's contributions as well as mine, and the sermon that had so eloquently portrayed his heart and character. I knew I had to get this done and I kept telling myself that I would be okay. I had been through so much already and was doing so well, and I knew by now that the way to complete healing and peace was to face and plow through the pain. I finally pulled myself together and actually enjoyed looking at some of the pictures we had displayed at the viewing and funeral service. When I got to the last bag and made my way down the layers of its contents there, on the very bottom of the bag, was Bill's belt. . . BAM! I'd hit a land mine! I felt like I had been hit by a two-by-four. I physically jolted back from what I had just discovered, not knowing how I was going to handle this. I stared at that belt and recalled how Bill had worn it every day when he was able to work but how it had just hung in his closet the last two years of his life. We had taken it to the funeral home, but because Bill had filled up with so much fluid at the end, it did not fit and we had to buy a new one. In a nano-second I was a sobbing mess. I almost could not take the belt out of the bag. But I knew I had to do it, so I forced myself to forge forward. I placed my hand back into the bag, picked the belt up, looked squarely at it, and said aloud, "Well, I'm crying anyway so this is the perfect time. *The closet issue gets addressed. It gets cleaned now!*"

With that, I headed back to Bill's closet and very slowly, gingerly opened the door. Other than the obvious white puffs of dust strips along the tops of every piece of clothing, everything was exactly as Bill had left it on the morning of Monday, April 26, 2010. That had been the last time he had entered that closet to dress before Jimmie left to go back home. I entered the closet crying really hard, my heart breaking all over again, and ran my hand over the hangers of his *sick clothes.* One by one, I pulled each item off its hanger and placed it in a large plastic bag, marking each piece with the tears streaming off my face. Hangers flew off the wooden bars and onto the floor as I made my way quickly through Bill's organized categories: sick clothes, work clothes, dress clothes, casual clothes. I could not linger at this task. It was every bit as painful as I had imagined it would be, and the job had to be done quickly and deliberately if I was going to be able to complete it. I knew if I did not finish this, it would be a very long time before I would be up to the task again. This was a one-time shot and I had to take full advantage of the moment. A few minutes after I had started the clean-out, Joe came over to work on some "honey do's." Hearing me cry, he came back to the closet and begged to do the work for me. I reiterated that *I* had to do this for *me*, as much as for his Dad. He came over to me and gave me a wonderfully loving hug and kiss then lingered nearby as I completed my mission, sobbing the entire time. There isn't a better son on planet Earth than my Joe!

When all items of clothing and shoes had been packed up, I asked Joe to please get them out of the house quickly and take them to the local junior high school where there is a drop box for clothing donations. He graciously complied and I sighed with relief knowing I had scaled, and triumphed over, the last hurdle of my grief work. As painful as that task was, it was also amazingly freeing and I was really surprised by that! I felt as if a huge weight had been lifted off my shoulders and that I could now soar to the heavens. I was finally completely unencumbered from the pain and it felt so very good! My heart, in fact, was already joyful just knowing that my grief work was officially over.

That evening before I ended my day, I opened that closet door which I had shut so Buddy Rose would not get into the things I had been storing on the floor. I looked around the closet, saw all the empty hangers and bare wooden poles, and felt peace. I knew Bill did not need those clothes anymore, and now I did not need them either. I had to smile.

∽

Summary

*C*oming back from the darkest places of the most painful grief journey I have ever encountered took a lot of incredibly hard work on my part. It took a deep, strong faith in, and complete reliance on God. I reached out and accepted the grief counseling offered to me by Hospice and have even found a new friend in my grief counselor, Donna. I participated in the Grief Recovery Method® group at the hospital where I work, which I now facilitate. And, I accepted support from family, friends, and co-workers. I even had to take some medication for a while and though I fought it initially, I did need it for this specific journey. Since my depression was situational, I am now completely free of all anti-depressants. I resolutely determined to keep fighting my way back. I refused to even consider giving up. There were times when I just dug my heels in and would not give in to the depression and darkness. Sometimes it felt as if I was clawing my way out of the pit, a millimeter at a time, but I kept clawing. This was the fight *of* my life *for* my life. And, I was willing to do everything I could to get that life back.

Oh, I still miss Bill—a lot! I always will. My heart will always ache for him. But, the pain, darkness, fear, and suffering are gone. I am enjoying life again, and am hopeful about my future. I am open to the "new possibilities" a very dear friend encouraged me to look for. And, that feels good—*really* good!

133

As a result of the hard work I was willing to do, I have been able to tenderly tuck Bill's love and the wonderful memories of our thirty-nine years together into that place in my heart marked "Bill." And they are there for me to retrieve whenever I need to feel him close. Sometimes I cry and other times I smile, but they are all the compilation of the sweet, sweet moments of a life with which God had so richly blessed us.

And one day, at some point in my future, I know I will see Bill again. I have no doubt that it will be a moment of pure, unadulterated joy to see him again, a moment I look forward to with great anticipation and a huge smile on my face just thinking about it! Until then, though, I will continue to enjoy all the blessings of my life while reaching out to help other hurting souls find their way back from the pain and suffering of profound loss.

Full Circle

On Monday, January 9, 2012, I went to work and told a dear friend about triumphing over my last hurdle. It had been an enormous success for me and I had to share it. How wonderful it is to have such great support and encouragement and to be so loved! I also realized that on that very day, January 9th, Bill and I had had our first date forty-one years before! Having told the story about cleaning out the closet made me realize how very blessed I am and how, because I am now completely unrestricted emotionally, I can open my heart to the new blessings God will send my way. That is an amazing place to be! And I thought about how, by being willing to do the incredibly hard work required for recovery from grief, I had come full circle. I had survived the most devastating journey of my life and become stronger for it. I have also been given a new direction of ministry through this experience.

I am happy. I am fulfilled. I am unbelievably blessed. And I can now offer healing to others out of the depths of my own profound pain. Life just does not get any better than that!

Your Journey

*Y*our journey through your grief will be different from mine. It will be your own unique journey. No one can tell you what you should or should not feel. No other person knows what is right for you. Only you will know that. This journey is a very individual one. I am here to tell you, however, that you do not have to be "stuck" in your grief. You do not have to stay in that dark, lonely, fearful, cold place. You do not have to live with anger or pain. There *is* life after death, and you *can* come back to it. There is not just one thing that works for everyone so you will have to find out what will work for you. And, it may not be just one thing that will do it. Like me, you may need several methods of help to bring you back. But, I encourage you to fight hard to work through the darkness. By all means, get the professional help a grief counselor can give you. The tools that I learned through the Grief Recovery Method® program were hugely instrumental in healing my heart, and I whole-heartedly recommend that program. Reach out to God for He *so* wants to love and care for you. There is nothing like feeling His love and presence within you, giving you the strength you need to get through the worst of the journey. Get medication from your doctor if you need it. The stress from this journey can really take its toll on you, so do not hesitate to accept the help the right medicine can provide for you. Remember, though, that as helpful as medication can be, it does not replace the work that is necessary to face and work through your pain. If you do not have a pet, this would be a good time to consider getting one. It is amazing how much love and joy even a small animal can bring to your heart. And, not only are they such great companions, but caring for them brings healing to you, as well. Finally, accept the support and help others offer, for this is not a journey you can make successfully on your own.

I hope and pray that as you have read the story of my personal journey, you will be encouraged to forge ahead to your own restoration. Then the pain of reliving my own grief will have been very well worth it!

Contacting the Author

To contact the author, e-mail her at <u>priscilla.boos@aol.com</u>.

Our Wedding, October 2, 1971

The Girls

My Favorite Smile

Buddy Rose

Bill's Sense of Humor—Comparing Ashlyn's Baby Sock with His

Bill and Me–2002

Joe and Vicki

CPSIA information can be obtained at www.ICGtesting.com
Printed in the USA
LVOW112252120612

285757LV00002B/3/P